GIRLS DON'T POOP

Lessons in Anatomy, Hygiene & Sexual Promiscuity

by

JEN ASHTON

Girls Don't Poop
Copyright © 2011 by Jen Ashton
Cover by Jen Ashton

ISBN-13: 978-1467927369
ISBN-10: 1467927368

*This book contains explicit material suited only for adults and is intended for those over 18 years of age.

BOOKS BY JEN ASHTON

Goddess On The Go: *A Guidebook to Becoming Irresistible*
Adonis On The Go: *A Guidebook to Becoming Irresistible*
My Teenage Heart
Turds in the Punch Bowl
Turds, Nerds and the Totally Absurd

SHORT STORIES

The Pleasure Diaries: *Six Sinfully Delicious Stories Volumes 1- 3*
Guilty Pleasures: *3 Pleasure Diaries in One*
Sexcapades: *Six Sizzling Short Stories Volume 1-3*
Sexy Tales: *3 Sexcapades in One*
Simply Irresistible Sex Stories Boxed Set
Pleasure Diaries and Sexcapades
Instant Erotica: *Six Perfectly Pleasurable Stories Volumes 1- 3*
Instant Pleasure: *3 Instant Eroticas in One*
Monstrous Love: *Six Tales of Pleasure and Peril*
Between the Sheets: *Erotica for Couples*
Into the Night: *Paranormal Sex Stories*
Strange Sex: *18 One Night Stands*
Tempting Her: *Lipstick Lesbian Stories*
Criminal Lust: *Stories of Crime and Passion*
Jen Ashton's Big Book of Sex
I Sleep with Bad Boys
The Bad Boy Chronicles

ANTHOLOGIES

Sweet Seductions
Dark Romances
Any Time. Any Place. *Volumes 1- 3*
Any Way You Like It

Contents:

Lesson #1: JESSICA IS FULL OF SHIT 15

Lesson #2: PRIMPIN' AIN'T EASY 37

Lesson #3: IT'S A GIRL THING. PERIOD. 53

Lesson #4: GROW YOUR ASSETS.. 67

Lesson #5: IN CASE OF EMERGENCY 81

Lesson #6: THE IMPORTANCE OF BROWNIE POINTS 93

Lesson #7: I MIGHT BE GOING TO HELL 107

Lesson #8: WATCH YOUR MOUTH 125

Lesson #9: EITHER WAY, I LOSE 137

PRELUDE TO ADULTHOOD 153

Lesson #10: DON'T THINK OUTSIDE THE BOX.................... 157

Lesson #11: FAKE IT TIL YOU MAKE IT 171

Lesson #12: REVENGE IS SWEET 185

Lesson #13: KNOW YOUR LIMIT... 197

Dedication

To the women in my life who made my journey to womanhood anything but normal.

Author's Note

This book is about growing up. I've always said the only people who can't joke about puberty, are the ones going through it. Twenty years later, I think I'm finally ready to talk.

It took me years to understand my own body, and more years again to accept and love it. But all those lessons, as you'll see, were hard fought and in some cases only barely won. So it is my hope that these stories will help others to come to appreciate their own journeys of self-discovery—traditional or not—and, if nothing else, have a few good laughs at my expense.

~ Jen Ashton

GIRLS DON'T POOP

FOREWORD

I grew up a typical Midwestern tomboy. I wore my brother's hand-me-downs and caught bugs with my bare hands. My favorite show was Gomer Pyle. I stole my mother's pie tins and made mud pies with worms inside to give to all the neighborhood boys as peace offerings in hopes they would play with me. I loved Star Wars. But I wanted to *be* Han Solo, not kiss him. I hung my Barbies by nooses and demanded that Santa bring me He-Man, Skeletor and the Castle of Greyskull instead. I shot bb guns and rode skateboards. I had a paper route and even saved my earnings one summer to buy the newest GT Pro Freestyle bike on the market. The only day of the year you could find me in a dress was Easter, and that's because I had to wear one or I would be grounded.

I was the middle child of three, born to conservative Christian parents in the heart of the Bible Belt. I had an older brother, who was like God to me because he got all the cool toys, bunk beds with plaid sheets and blue walls in his room. His closet was full of awesome boy games like Rock 'em Sock 'em Robots and Battleship. But the best thing about his closet wasn't the toys, it was the autographed poster on the back of the door of Hall and Oates from my brother's first rock concert. It's no wonder I fought hard to share a room with him when our little sister was born.

Sharing a room with my brother made us two peas in a pod. When he dressed like a cowboy for Halloween, I was an Indian. When he was Snoopy, I was Woodstock. When he was a sheriff, I was a hippie. We shared clothes and toys and even haircuts. At the time, my mom was putting herself through beauty school with the money she made from hosting Tupperware parties and teaching makeup classes at the YMCA. Unfortunately, that made my brother and me hair guinea pigs, and now with a third child to care for, I believe she just opted for something simple and universal; the oh-so-popular bowl cut. Yes, we both had one of those hideous *don'ts* and there are plenty of pictures to prove it. I now know it was no happy accident that my brother and I looked like Dumb and Dumber for far longer than it was trendy, if in fact, it ever was.

Things didn't change much when I became a teenager. There was enough money to dress me like a girl, but by then I was smart enough to just combine my shopping allowance with my brother's and hit up the boys department with twice as much cash. I still had my GT Pro Freestyle, which I used to deliver papers each day, and I took the trucks off my old skateboards and turned them into snowboards. I graduated from catching bugs to catching animals and made out with my pillow instead of making mud pies. I had my own room and my Barbies were now having sex with my He-Man figures. Well, at least as best they could without any genitalia. My hair had grown longer and I still loved Star Wars the same; only now, it was less about my dreams of fighting the Galactic Empire aboard the Millennium Falcon and more about the warm tingly feeling I experienced between my legs every time Han Solo appeared on the screen.

My parents eventually divorced. My brother and I, along with all of our clothes, moved in with our dad, where I would live out most of my remaining years as a minor. This probably didn't help me to embrace my femininity any better while I was blossoming under my corduroy jeans and flannel shirts. My father worked "late" most nights and my brother had a car. It wasn't cool to hang out with his little sis anymore. Needless to say, not only was I sans a mother figure for awhile, but the male influences in my life were absent too. There was no one to tell me about the birds and the bees, my changing body or the warm tingle. However, that also meant there was no one around to stop me from watching late night Cinemax with my hands under the blankets, purchasing creams and products from the back of Cosmo, or looking like a whore when I left the house to loiter around the fly-by-night carnival in the Target parking lot. It was a long and lonely journey to self discovery. It's no wonder I turned to magazines, friends and neighbors to learn about becoming a woman.

I eventually blossomed. And, to make my mother proud, I wear dresses all the time now. But being a woman didn't come naturally for me, and my journey wasn't without a lot of warped advice, innocent misunderstandings and hilarious adventures. Needless to say, after three decades of trying to make sense of it all, I think I've got the hang of this feminine thing now. Here is my story—from breast cream to fart machines, and all of the characters in between—the tried and true lessons of my youth that steered me toward becoming the woman I am today.

Lesson #1:

JESSICA IS FULL OF SHIT

Jessica has been my best friend for as long as I can remember. She talked like a sailor and walked like a man, even in the third grade. With country in her blood and an invisible horse saddled up between her legs, she was as manly as an eight year old girl could be. She lacked all things effeminate, which made us a perfect match. Rather than sundresses and bobby socks, we could be found wearing cut-off jean shorts and leather jackets, hiding behind the school bus holding a spitting contest. When the boys would try to out-spit our loogies, Jessica would puff up her chest and launch one twice as far, following up her winning shot with some hillbilly phrase like, "This dog's too old to get fucked by the puppies." There was nothing not to love about her.

Jessica and I were joined at the hip for years. We rode bikes, skated around the neighborhood and played in the mud together. We never wore shoes and always got into trouble. We played outside from sun-up to sun-down every day, rain or shine. She helped me with my paper route and I helped her with her appetite. Every day after school, we would load up my paper bag with rolled newspapers and throw it over my handlebars. Jessica would jump on the back pegs and we would ride over to an adjacent neighborhood to deliver them. Afterward, I would steer us over to the local grocery store for a snack.

"You hungry?" I would always ask, even though I already knew the answer.

"Yep," she always responded with her husky voice.

We would walk around the produce section, sampling free cheese, crackers, fruit and cookies. You would've thought we were poor and our parents didn't feed us. After the first lap, we often ran to the restroom, switch shirts and hats and went back for round two. Surely, no one would recognize us as the two girls dressed like boys who gobbled up half of the free samples just ten minutes before. Nope. Never. Unfortunately, we could never fool the bakery ladies, and they chased us off...every single time.

Once full of hors d'oeuvres, we would head over to the magazine rack to load up on all the

Jen Ashton

Tiger Beat gossip and check out the new boy's fashions circa 1987. One day, while stealing a centerfold of Joe Elliott from Def Leppard, the cheese finally got to me.

"Hey Jess, I gotta go to the bathroom."

"Too much information," she replied, never taking her eyes off the poster of Bret Michaels that she was ogling.

"Come with me," I whispered. "I've gotta poop real bad."

"Impossible," she responded.

By this time I was wriggling around in my jean shorts, confused by her response and running short on time. "What do you mean, *impossible*? I think the cheese upset me stomach, I gotta go poop. Just put Bret down and come with me."

"Impossible," she said again, turning toward me and looking at me over the top of her magazine.

Suddenly, my feelings were hurt. There I was, her best friend, requesting her company in the restroom while I sat on the shitter and she was so fixated on her poster of Poison that she was turning me down. What kind of best friend was she? She could see the urgency as I stood there, holding myself as I danced around trying to keep my insides inside. And it was obvious that our friendship meant more to me than my rumbling tummy and clenched butt cheeks because I hadn't left yet.

"Why is it so impossible for you to come with me?" I yelled in my best whisper voice, trying to remain calm so that my stomach muscles didn't accidentally push anything out preemptively.

It was clear that Jessica was handling the situation more calmly than me. She stood there, in her jean shorts and jacket, with a ripped concert tee and a button that read *I heart Brandon,* staring at me. I was waddling back and forth, warming up with panic. Then, she looked me straight in the eye and told me something I had never heard before.

"Girls don't poop."

"What?!?!" I was confused and growing dizzy from running around in small circles.

"It's impossible, because girls don't poop," she reiterated.

"You're dumb," I told her. "Of course they do. Everybody poops!"

Jen Ashton

"I don't."

"Then where does your food go?" I asked. By this time I was turning red and I knew I couldn't hold it much longer. Still, the conversation was more important than my bowel movements.

"Our bodies absorb it as fat," she educated me. It made sense, a little. Practically every woman I knew *was* on the bigger side. She continued. "Then we sweat it out."

I tried to process this information as best a ten year old could. I knew I had been pooping for years. I suddenly began to question whether I was a girl or not. Talking as softly as I could, I repeated her lesson back to her. "So girls don't poop?" I asked.

"Nope."

"Because?"

"We don't have buttholes," she said matter-of-factly.

Either she was lying or I was a boy, because I had a butthole and it was straining to stay closed at that moment.

"Girls don't poop and they don't fart," she added.

"They don't fart either?!?!" I asked frantically, pursing my lips and clinching my teeth as I bent down in the aisle. "Then what do they do?" My patience was wearing thin and my butt was sweating.

"We burp."

"Well that's a relief!" I said sarcastically. At least I got that part right. I danced around hastily, trying to put it all together as my large intestine filled to the brim. I knew I was a girl, but I also had a butthole. I pooped and I farted, at least to the best of my knowledge. And although I dressed like a boy and played with boy toys and had a best friend who acted like a man, I wasn't totally sure I really wanted to be a boy. But one thing I did know for sure, I didn't want to get fat. So I repeated the lesson one more time, just to make sure I understood.

"So girls don't poop. They sweat?" It suddenly seemed I may be a girl after all since I was sweating profusely by that point.

Jen Ashton

No," she corrected me. "Girls don't poop. They glitter."

I almost shit my pants right then and there; right in front of the magazine rack. I couldn't take it anymore. I was sweating like a girl, but I sure had to poop like a boy.

"I gotta go, Jess," I panicked. "Just come with me. Please!"

Jessica pulled the staples from the center of her magazine and ripped out the Poison poster. As she folded it up and shoved it inside her jean jacket, she finally accompanied me to the restroom where I ran inside and glittered…a lot.

*****

By fifth grade, we were still tight like spandex. Ever the tomboys, we spent our summer days venturing off into the woods pretending to be Tom Sawyer and Huck Finn, scouting out new territories and causing all kinds of mischief. One afternoon, we were walking the top of a wooden fence between neighborhoods, imagining we were in some far-off land discovering foreign soil, when we encountered our first naked man. Jessica spotted him first.

"Don't look now," she whispered, "but there's a naked man in that window."

"What window?" I asked, turning instinctively to scan the apartments facing the fence.

"I said, don't look!" she shouted, pushing me hard.

I fell off the fence into the bushes below. "Ouch!" I screamed, feeling a sharp pain in my ankle. Among the branches, I reached down to hold my leg and immediately started crying. I was hurt.

"Shhh," Jessica shushed me. "He'll hear us!"

"Who?"

"The naked man," she told me. Jumping to the ground and crouching next to me, she pointed through the fence to a window on the other side. "He's right there."

Wiping the tears from my eyes and leaning forward to a get a glimpse, I saw him. "Gross!" I exclaimed, subsequently placing my own hand over my mouth. "I've never seen one."

"A man?" Jessica snapped.

"No," I said coyly. "A—you know—a thingy."

"A thingy?" she mocked me. "You mean a penis?"

"Shhh," I hushed her, rustling in the bush and looking back through the fence. The man was standing in his window, naked as a jaybird. We could see him pretty clearly through the screen. He stood there stroking himself. Then he walked away for a minute. "What is he doing?"

"Peeing," Jessica assured me.

"Then why is he rubbing it?"

"He's not rubbing it. He's pumping it. That's how boys get the pee out."

"Gross!" I was utterly amused, aside from my disgust. "How does our pee come out then?" I was genuinely curious to know the answer and Jessica always seemed to know more than me about people's bodies. I chalked it up to growing up in the country and working with animals.

Before she could answer, the man exited his patio door and walked out onto his balcony, not more than ten feet above our heads. I had a direct view of his hairy penis and started giggling. The man heard us and covered himself.

"Who's there?" he yelled out, returning to his apartment.

We wrestled around in the bush as I tried to get up, only to find out I couldn't put any weight on my foot.

"Here," Jess hurried. "Hold on!" She pulled me up and draped my arms around her neck to carry me away. She had the brawn of ten mules. "You're heavier than a box of rocks," she told me. Dragging me behind her, we limped through the thicket as fast as we could, laughing, yet scared out of our wits. Suddenly, we heard a door slam behind us and I saw the man, still unclothed, running along the other side of the fence toward us.

"He's coming!" I shouted. "Run!"

Hobbling at mach speed, we ran through the tall weeds and trees until we found an opening that veered away from the fence. Screaming like girls at the top of our lungs, we made our escape and lost him. When we finally reached her house, she helped me elevated my ankle and put some ice on it. We laid there swapping penis stories and catching our breaths.

Jen Ashton

"That was disgusting!" I told her. "I saw it bouncing when he was running after us."

"Shut up. You couldn't see it."

"Yes I could!" I promised. "It was floppy. Not like it was in the window."

"That's because he got all the pee out," she insisted.

After giggling for awhile, it became evident that we were both turning red and not from embarrassment. Both of us were beginning to itch like crazy.

"Oh shit," Jess finally said. "You're covered in poison ivy!"

"Oh my God!" I screamed, realizing that she, too, was covered in a growing rash. "Do you have any Calamine lotion?" I asked, attempting to let my foot down to help.

"Don't move, I'll see what my mom has." She disappeared into the bedroom and returned quickly with a white bottle. "There's no label, but it's lotion!"

She lathered the lotion on both of our legs and we settled in to feel its soothing relief. That never came. In fact, it was the opposite. Within minutes, my legs flared up like they were on fire. I couldn't get up fast enough and started panicking.

"Jess, hurry! Help me up. I gotta get this stuff off my legs! Oh my God, what was that stuff? Hurry!"

Jessica was in a panic of her own, running around fanning her own burning legs. She grabbed me and dragged me into the bathroom where she ran the bathwater and piled us both inside the tub.

We were both screaming and laughing, unaware of what was happening. An equal amount of fear and humor raced through my veins as I washed my legs vigorously. Squished in the tub with my manly friend behind me, fiendishly rubbing my legs with soap and water, I began to notice something floating in the water around me. It was dark and coarse. *What the hell is that?*

Suddenly, Jessica screamed.

"My hair!!!"

I turned around and looked at her head. There was nothing wrong with her hair. My eyes scanned her over until they reached her perfectly shiny, smooth legs.

Jessica's scream woke her older sister who came running into the bathroom to make sure we were okay. Standing over us with her hands on her hips, she stared at us in disappointment through her glasses.

"Jess!" she yelled, picking up the empty bottle of lotion that was lying on the rug in front of the tub. "You used all my Nair?!?!"

Sure enough, I looked down to find that my legs, too, were hairless and smooth. My mom was going to kill me! I wasn't allowed to shave my legs yet, and there was no way I was going to return home with shaved legs, let alone poison ivy, a sprained ankle and stories of a naked man.

"Jess," I winced, "can I stay the night?"

*****

By sixth grade, Jessica and I were attending different schools. She had returned to her roots in the country and I continued my education in the suburbs. We still got to together on the weekends to play. One afternoon while fishing off her father's dock, Jess told me about her new schoo!.

"How's school?" I asked her.

"It sucks."

"Why?"

"I have to take Ag."

"What's Ag?" I asked.

"Some farmer class."

"Why's it called Ag?"

"Because people in the country don't know how to spell *farm*."

"Wow, that's weird."

"I know," she agreed. "And they're so dumb they still teach about China in Social Studies."

"They teach us about China at my school, too. Are they not supposed to?"

"No, that's old school. Everybody knows China isn't a real place."

"It's not?"

Jen Ashton

"No dummy! It doesn't even exist."

"I never knew that." I told her, tugging on my line.

"You didn't? I've known that all along."

"You've known what?" I was now thoroughly amused by her scholarly wisdom and the archaic teachings of my junior high school.

"I've always known that China wasn't real. It's just a place that you dig for in your sandbox."

This information didn't go over very well when I returned to school on Monday to advise my geography teacher of her old-school ways.

*****

In high school, Jessica and I were still inseparable. Wearing our flannel shirts and cut-off jeans, we still resembled Tom Sawyer and Huck Finn; except we had boobs. And now we wore socks with our Birkenstocks. We were into drugs, house parties and The Grateful Dead. We lived in a predominantly white, affluent community that frowned upon our suburban hippy fashions and lackadaisical attitudes. To be honest, it was mostly the weed that was to blame, but our parents were none-the-wiser.

My house was no stranger to teenage parties back in the day. Whenever there was a weekend, there was a party. All the kids from our high school would show up, and even kids from neighboring schools and counties. We'd have everyone from country bumpkins to private school yuppies hopped up on THC in my bedroom on any given Friday night. We were a bunch of white hippy kids who could afford the good stuff, and that not only meant we were high—really high—but that we also had a supply. And for the most part, we were willing to share.

Jessica never missed a party, even if she was too high to make it. She only lived a few houses down and if she was too stoned to walk, she would get a ride. This happened one summer evening when my house was full of new "alternative" kids from a more urban town called Broad Ripple. Jessica arrived just as they all shuffled in with their blue hair and nose rings, wallet chains and pale skin; save one.

"Did you see him?" Jessica inquired secretly.

"Who?" I asked, alarmed by her panic.

Jen Ashton

"*Him!*"

"Him who?" I was still confused.

"Jim Watson."

"Jim who?"

"Jim Watson," she insisted, talking sharply with her teeth clenched.

"I don't know who that is," I reminded her.

"The black man," she whispered.

Jessica was raised in the sticks. To boot, we were also in the heart of the Bible Belt and our folk—the rednecks—were known to be a bit prejudice. All her life she had never known a black person, nor had she ever seen one up close and personal. And now there was one standing in my kitchen, scaring the Be-Jesus out of her just by being there.

To make matters worse, the only black man Jessica was familiar with before that night was Jim Watson from Huckleberry Finn. And the fact that he was a freed slave in Mark Twain's story didn't help her to adopt a modern view. The poor girl had been raised around every stereotype and racial profile of black people and had nothing more to go on. When they say ignorance is bliss, I don't think they were referring to Jessica. There was nothing blissful about her disposition at that moment. Standing there in all her brawn—a masculine woman in the midst of puberty who chewed tobacco and walked around saddle-sore—my best friend cowered for the first time.

"He scares me," she shivered.

"Why does he scare you?" I was intrigued by her statement, but her answer was far more interesting.

"They have no bones," she whispered.

"Who?"

"Black people."

"What?!?! You're high. Who told you that?"

"No one. I just know it."

"That's ridiculous. All people have bones."

"Black people don't," she stated again, snooping around the corner to see where Jim

Watson disappeared to. "You better watch him, Jen. He might rob the place."

"What?!?! Jessica, lay of the weed. You're acting nuttier than a squirrel turd right now. Just because he's black doesn't mean he's gonna rob my house. "

"I'm serious," she muffled under her breath, acting like a paranoid Sherlock Holmes. "I can't stay here. He scares me."

"Because he doesn't have bones?"

"Exactly. Think about it. That's how they can jump so high."

"So black people jump high because they don't have bones? I'm not following you." At this point, I needed to be higher than I was to comprehend her staggering claim. I reached for a joint and a lighter.

"They're made out of cartilage," she informed me.

"Cartilage, like from your nose?" I inquired, taking a hit and holding it in.

"Like sharks," she told me. "It's more flexible than bone. That's how they jump so high."

"Are you serious?" I coughed and blew out what was left of the smoke I had been holding in my lungs.

She continued, whispering softly, "That's also why they don't die when you shoot them."

"Oh c'mon, Jess! Where do you get this bullshit?"

"It's true," she swore, looking around to reassure her security. "Watch yourself. I'm tellin' ya, if he robs you, Jim Watson won't go down if you have to shoot him."

"What are *you* smokin' girl?" I asked half-joking, but she didn't laugh.

"I can't stay. I gotta get outta here."

Two hours later Jessica returned, still a little skittish. But I promised her that Jim Watson had left the party. As she made her way down the stairs to my basement bedroom, a dark man walked up behind her and shoved a candy bar in her back.

"Don't move!" he shouted.

Jen Ashton

"Oh my God," Jessica whimpered. Her voice barely escaped her lips as they trembled with fear. "Oh my God, *oh my God*!!! What do you want?"

"I want your money," he growled in her ear. She tried to turn around, but he shoved the candy bar deeper into back. "Put your hands up!"

Jessica put her hands up and begged for her life. "Please, sir…" she pleaded.

"Please, *Jim*," he corrected her.

"Please, Jim…" she begged.

"Please, Jim *Watson*!" he groaned, jabbing her again in the back.

All of the color drained from Jessica's face instantaneously and I believe that, in that moment, she learned that girls *do*, in fact, poop because she most definitely shit her pants on my stairway that night.

I laughed so hard I almost died of a heart attack. She was full of shit after all.

*Jessica is now married to a black man and has three beautiful babies by him. They all have bones.

Girls Don't Poop

Lesson #2:

PRIMPIN' AIN'T EASY

I've wanted to be a model since I received my first compliment.

"Aw, isn't she precious," my grandmother swooned.

That's all I needed to hear. It was in my blood. I was born to model and I was determined to get a head start on the other girls. So, it's no surprise that photos exist of me posing in my crib naked with a mink throe. All I was missing was a little lipstick. I was such an amateur then. But flash forward six years and I would finally get my chance to go pro.

One afternoon while I was reorganizing my Star Wars figures in my new Darth Vader case, my mom knocked on the bedroom door.

"Jennie?" she asked sweetly. "How would you like to model tonight at my Tupperware party?"

I almost pissed in my Dungarees. Maybe there *was* an innate desire to be a girl somewhere under my striped Izod polo and dark denim jeans after all. Or not. Looking back, my mom probably just wanted to get me into a dress, but to me, this was my chance to strut my stuff. I had fantasies of becoming a big time Christmas catalog model. Every December I would flip through the pages of the Sears Catalog, circling images of the latest boy's fashion—Oshkosh overalls, Michael Jackson Thriller jacket, soccer cleats—you name it, I was all about putting in years of hard work at Tupperware parties, family functions, or neighborhood picnics to earn my way up the ranks to model it someday. And now, here was my chance. It was an offer I couldn't refuse.

My eyes lit up with excitement and I smiled bigger than ever before. Little did I know then, that this would be the beginning of a string of modeling assignments to earn my merits. And they would all start with, "Jennie, would you like to model for me tonight?" Those few words would soon take a strange toll—from sheer eagerness to pay my dues to absolute horror when I looked in the mirror—all for the sake of chasing my dreams to be a male model.

"Come down to the kitchen once you've put your toys away," my mom instructed. "I'll show you what you'll need to do."

Jen Ashton

I showed up a few minutes later wearing my best plaid shirt, still rocking my Dungarees. My mom pulled back my hair and asked me to sit on a chair in the middle of the room. She draped a cape over my shoulders and started to apply makeup to my face. It was the eighties, so she caked on the blue eye shadow and red lipstick; a trend she would repeat over and over and over again on my poor little face every time we went to Sears for family photos. And though I forced a smile for the sake of not getting grounded, I knew in my heart that the makeup was never going to increase my chances of being recognized by the photographer as the next face of "Boys Size 8-10."

When she was done making me look like a clown, my mom opened the cupboards to reveal a stockpile of Tupperware containers filled with pickles. I'm not talking about a few pickles. And I'm not talking about a few containers. My mom had spent the greater part of the summer tending to our new garden, hoarding cucumbers for her pickle collection. If there was a natural disaster, we would've surely had enough bread and butter pickles to last us a decade. Maybe more. But that wasn't the idea. My mom had skillfully executed a plan to market her pickles by presenting them inside the Tupperware that evening. She was a genius. I definitely got my entrepreneurial spirit from her. Good genes in her genius.

"Now all you have to do is this," she began, holding the Tupperware filled with pickles in one hand as she presented it with her other hand like the models did on Price Is Right. She made it look effortless.

The ladies shuffled in about 6:30pm. They all gathered in the living room, sipping tea and snacking on pickles. My mom made me wait in the kitchen. She wanted me to make a grand entrance in all my made up glory, walk around to each woman modeling the Tupperware and then return to pick up the next item. It seemed simple enough and I knew I had what it took to rock this party. I was even wearing a dab of my dad's cologne.

The women all gasped when I turned the corner, though they quickly fell silent and faked their smiles. They were all probably wondering what the hell I had done to myself.

"Doesn't she look pretty?" my mom coaxed them. "This is my daughter, Jennie. She will be modeling all of our Tupperware this evening."

Each woman hesitantly agreed, whispering under their breaths. These Midwest Bible bangers clearly didn't know a model when they saw one. I walked right past the first few sneers, grinning big to show the hole in my smile left from the first tooth I had lost just the week before.

"You look so grown up," one lady remarked, but what she meant to say was, "Wow, you look like a whore, sweetie, let's go upstairs and wash that crap off your face." I just smiled and curtsied.

"And what do we have *here*?" another lady asked, referring to my face and not the Tupperware.

"You look like a little Madonna," one heckler commented, though Like a Virgin was her only song out that year. And that didn't exactly make her a public saint.

The whole house smelled like pickles and plastic, and the women that evening all lied to my face. I know that now. They told me I looked pretty—even though I didn't—and they each glared at me under their matronly, untrimmed brows while they ate pickles and ogled over plastic containers, feeling sorry for me. It was so condescending. But honestly, I knew what they were up to. Nope. No way. I had that shit in the bag. Though a few of them looked more mannish than me, they were all too old to win my spot in the 8-10 category.

Jen Ashton

*****

"Jennie, would you like to model for me tonight?" Here we go again, another chance to pay my dues. One step closer to modeling for the men's department.

My mom was resourceful. When the Tupperware and pickle thing failed to continue producing a profit, she turned to makeup. Maybe that was the plan all along. Man, she was smart. She had me modeling her talent at that first party and I didn't even know it. But Tupperware parties were beneath her now. She had signed up for a company called Beauty for All Seasons and she was holding classes at the YMCA. My mom was big time.

Beauty for All Seasons consisted of a three part process. First, my mom draped a ring of fabric color samples over your shoulder to assess which "season" you were. The four color palettes represented the color of each seasons. For instance, *winter* was bold and bright. *Spring* was pastel. Fall, the ugly puke greens and baby shit oranges. You get the idea. Anyway, once she determined what *season* you were, she would counsel you on a specific wardrobe. Bless you if you were a fall. After that, my mom would open her bag of makeup and apply a disastrous amount of seasonal hues on

Jen Ashton

your once pleasant face. Again, bless you if you were a fall. (These poor women always walked out looking like a diaper exploded on their eyes.)

Though I was working my way up to the Sears catalog, I was never too good for the Y. This was going to be a great place for me to showcase my talents. I accepted my mom's offer with sheer enthusiasm. And this was a step up. She had asked me to be a real model this time. I was going to sit in front of the class and let her apply makeup on my face to show the other women all her application tips. Deep inside, I knew that all those little boys in the magazines had to wear some sort of makeup when they modeled. The boys in my neighborhood didn't have perfect faces like that. And their lips weren't that pink either. So, I convinced myself this makeup class was alright. *All male models sit in the makeup chair,* I told myself.

We arrived at the Y a little early so my mom could set up. A blossoming artist among other things, I was further solicited for my talents.

"You're good at art, Jennie. Would you draw an eye on the chalkboard for me?"

My skills proved valuable. Looking up at that eye when I finished, I knew it was the best damn eye I had ever drawn. Needless to say, I was feeling quite confident before the class even started. But that was all a little premature. I had no idea what I was in for.

"Good evening, ladies," my mother said, welcoming the class. "This is my daughter, Jennie. She will be modeling for us tonight."

"Hi, Jennie," they all chimed together.

"Welcome to Beauty for All Seasons. Tonight I will be showing you how to determine what season you are, followed by how to select a wardrobe based on those colors." My mom pulled the color swatches from her bag and held them up one by one, finishing with the puke colors. "And though Jennie is a *winter*," she dictated, laying the fabric over my shoulder, "it looks like most of you in here are *autumns*, so I'm going to go ahead and play with the fall colors on her tonight."

*****

In the fourth grade, I sat in the back of the bus with all the other boys. We threw paper airplanes at the other students and sang the latest heavy metal hits by Megadeth and Metallica. My hair was long, for once, and parted in the middle, so it was easy to throw around when I played air guitar in our make-

Jen Ashton

believe thrasher band. Row 13—that was the place to be.

That year there was a new boy in town. He lived in my neighborhood and his bus stop was the stop after mine. He was immediately welcomed into the band and he took up residency in Row 14, right behind me. I couldn't help but keep turning around to stare at him. He had tan skin and big brown eyes. His haircut was a little funny, but it wasn't anything my mom couldn't fix. (She was in beauty school already.) Despite that one shortcoming, he had a wicked smile and he made me feel shy. After a few days of dueting together on our own version of For Whom the Bell Tol!s, I finally mustered up the courage to strike a conversation with him.

Turning around and clinching the green vinyl as I looked over the top of my seat, my voice squeaked. "You wanna play after school?" I asked him.

"I can't," he told me. "My dad says I have to do my homework."

"Oh, okay," I conceded. I started to turn around and sit back down in my seat in utter heartache.

"But maybe after my homework is finished," he

added.

And that's how Jason and I became friends. We bonded fast. I always passed my stop and got off the bus with him. We would walk along the golf course in or neighborhood for a few minutes after school—talking and laughing, flirting and chasing each other—before he had to do his homework. He would call me when he was finished and, if I was lucky, we would play some more before dinner. It didn't take long before I was in love; the fourth grade kind.

I had the biggest crush on my new best friend. He embodied every single thing I loved about a boy. He was every reason I wanted to be one! I loved the way his eyes lit up when he laughed, yet he still tried to be tough. I like the way he looked at me, even when he was trying to hide his emotions. He was funny. He was cute. He played in the dirt and he could do a front indo on his dirt bike. He was awesome on a skateboard, too, and even taught me a few tricks. We were like two peas in a pod.

It wasn't long before I was writing Jason's name on every folder I owned. Jason, in bubble letters. Jason, inside a heart with an arrow shooting through it. Jason, with hearts on either side of his name. Jason, Jason, Jason. I fantasized about him even when he was walking next to me. He was my best friend, my crush, my...dream boy. With every step of our feet, every pedal of our bike, I wished he would just ask me already. What was taking him so long? When was he going to ask me to *go with him*?

The days came and went and before I knew it, months had passed and we were still just friends. I still walked him home like the gentleman I was, every day after school. We still rode bikes together and rocked out on the school bus. Nothing had changed. I was almost ready to give up, but I had one last trick up my sleeve. I realized that maybe Jason didn't think of me as a *girl*. So one day after school, I hatched a plan to make him see me as one and went home to tell my mom.

"Mom! Mom!" I yelled as I ran in the house. "I need you to make me pretty!"

"Perfect timing, Jennie. I just learned something new in school today and I wanted to try it on you anyway. Would you like to be my model?"

I should've been afraid—especially after my bowl-cut years and having my face shat on at the YMCA—but I let her work her magic anyway. Two hours and 300 tiny little curlers later, I had a perm. Not just any perm, the tightest poodle perm you've ever seen. And that wasn't the worst of it. My mom thought it was a good idea to cut me a few bangs beforehand. So there I was, my long hair cinched into a solid bob, with frizzy bangs that resembled a pair of poodle balls.

"Oh, Jennie," my mom winced after my hair was dry. "I'm so sorry." There was a long pause as she examined her creation. "It doesn't look *that* bad. It'll grow out."

By the tone in her voice I knew my "something new she learned in school" hadn't quite been executed properly. I had a feeling my mom was going to flunk beauty school. In the meantime, I needed to find a mirror.

"Shit!" I shouted, a little too loud. "God dammit, Mom!" She had never heard me curse before and now I was unleashing every fowl word I knew. "What the hell? How am I supposed to go to school like this tomorrow?"

"Honey, I'm sorry. Maybe I shouldn't have used such small rods. We can try washing it after school to see if it relaxes a little. If not, it'll grow out. Don't worry."

"Don't worry? Don't *worry*?!!! How can you

say don't worry when it looks like you gave me grandma's hairdo?!!! I'm ruined! *Ruined*!!!" I ran to my room and slammed the door.

The next day, I walked down the middle of the bus to Row 13. My shoulders sloped and my back hunched, I was ruined, mortified, humiliated. I threw my backpack on the seat and laid down on it, hiding from everyone. I wasn't sure how I was going to get through the day. But first, I had to get through revealing my hair to Jason. As we turned the corner down his street, I tried to put on my best happy face. Without smiling. My perm made my face look fat. I sat up and tried to convey a bit of confidence.

The doors opened and one by one the students boarded until the very last one was on and the doors closed. *Where was Jason*? Phew! Maybe I had dodged the most humiliating moment of my life. Maybe I still had time to fix my hair after school and save myself the embarrassment.

Nope. Here he came, running beside the bus, yelling for the driver to open the doors. He ran up the steps and walked toward me, never making eye contact. I thought maybe he was trying to be nice by not making a spectacle of my hair *don't*. Wrong.

"Oh my *Gawd*!!!" he gasped, finally locking

eyes with me. "What the fuck happened to your hair?!!!"

Now my face was fat *and* red. I was so embarrassed. I sunk into my seat and hid my head in the proverbial sand. I never wanted to show my face again. But then I felt a tap on my shoulder. I turned and looked up. It was Jason, leaning over my seat. I hoped he had changed his tune, realizing I was hurt by it. I hoped he'd look past my hair and still see my inner beauty. I hoped he would comfort me in my time of need and be the best friend I knew him to be. I waited for his words of comfort.

"You know," he said. "I was going to ask you to go with me today. But not now. You look *so* ugly!"

I was devastated. The moment I had been waiting for all year—the moment I had tried to coax with my terrible plan to look pretty—the moment where I finally became Jason's girlfriend—had been thwarted by the worst hairdo I have ever had. Even worse than the bowl. I was literally channeling Bob Ross. So, as I walked into school that morning with a freshly broken heart, it didn't even faze me when I read the banner above the front door.

TODAY IS PICTURE DAY!

Jen Ashton

Jen Ashton

Girls Don't Poop

Jen Ashton

Lesson #3:

IT'S A GIRL THING. PERIOD.

My brother and I were latchkey kids. While Mom was in beauty school, we often found ourselves unsupervised for several hours at a time on school days. This became a prime opportunity for my brother to bully me. We would race off the school bus to the kitchen, fighting over the snack drawer. He always won, therefore declaring him King of the Twinkies. He hoarded those delicious yellow sponge cakes—for years—and left me no choice but to settle for second fiddle; the Ding Dongs. I didn't mind so much. I loved their chocolaty goodness and creamy filling. At least I still got to partake in that scrumptious Hostess cream filling. It tasted so good. This was the age of innocence. The time when I actually just ate my Ding Dong, instead of staring at it first, seriously considering how they actually got that white fluffy stuff inside the holes.

Everyone knows Ding Dongs paired well with an ice cold Coke. And like any other product of eighties pop culture, my after school snack was not complete without two unique cultural experiences. One: removing the "pop top" of my soda can without breaking the tiny ring on it. (I was told these little collectibles could be exchanged for kisses from boys. So I proudly saved them all in a Ziploc baggy, waiting for the day to cash them in on my crush.) And two: smashing the wrapper of my Ding Dong on the counter into some abstract piece of flattened, tin foil origami art.

"Hmm? Looks like a hippo today," I said to myself one afternoon, squinting my eyes and stretching my imagination, "sitting on a cloud with a sword in its hand."

Speaking of swords, it was time to get out He-Man and a Skeletor. It wasn't uncommon for me to get at least one battle in before my mom got home. But that particular afternoon, while playing on the floor in my parent's bedroom, I decided I wanted to wage a full-on Masters of the Universe war. The only problem was that I didn't have enough action figures. I needed more soldiers. After searching the house over, I ended up with He-Man, his tiger, his castle, Skeletor, two Barbies and a Ken doll. Not the most desirable army, but it would have to do. Now, all I needed was some weapons.

Skeletor had a staff. He-Man had his sword. I needed something awesome for the Barbies. Hmm? Where could I find something cool to use as a gun? My little girl eyes turned to my mother's bathroom. Surely, she would have something in her makeup case that would make a great gun. I crawled along the floor, setting my eyes on the cabinet under the sink. When I finally opened the doors, I was met with an array of womanly products; perfumes, makeup, curling irons, lotions and potions galore. And just beyond all the bottles, far in the back, hiding under a bag of makeup, was a white box with the letters o.b.

"O.B.? What the heck is that?" I asked aloud. The only "O.B." I knew up to that point was Obi Wan Kenobi. Surely my mom wasn't hiding him under her sink!

Pushing all the other products aside, I reached deep for the little box and retrieved it without a hitch. I lifted the lid and peeked inside. No Obi Wan. All that was inside was a few white bullets shrink-wrapped in plastic. I had no idea what they were, but they would make great guns!

"O.B." I repeated. "Official bazooka!"

That's all I needed. I grabbed the white bazookas and secured one under the arm of each

Barbie. Ken had two. I was prepped and ready for war.

"You're going down!" I announced in a low voice that was supposed to be Ken's. "Feel the wrath of my O.B.!"

Skeletor cowered in the distance as imaginary missiles shot from the cannon of my O.B. and destroyed the drawbridge of The Castle of Grayskull. "Die, Skeletor! Die!" I shouted, making high-pitched shooting sounds that sounded like, "Pew, pew pew!"

"Jennie?" Her voice scared the BeJesus out of me. "What are you doing?!?!"

I looked up to find my mom, standing over me, with a confused look on her face. She had come home from beauty school early that day to find me torturing Skeletor with her tampons. And I was in for the lesson of my life.

*****

An hour later, I was still sitting on the bathroom rug in my mother's bathroom while she kindly explained women's anatomy, periods and tampons to her ten year old daughter. The problem was, I was ten. I had no idea what she was talking about, nor how to decipher that strange drawing of a woman on the back of the o.b. box. It didn't even look like a woman. It was just curved lines with a tube in the middle.

"See Jennie," my mom continued, "this is where the tampon goes."

By that time I wasn't listening anyway. Once we passed the blood talk, I was done. I just sat there, pretending to listen while she kept pointing to the cross section of the woman's womb on the box. Curved lines and a tube. It didn't make sense any way I looked at it. So I gave up trying to stretch my imagination. To be quite frank, the idea that there was a tube inside me was confusing. When I looked down at my body in the shower, all I saw was a vertical line; no tube, just a slit. And that line had been there for as long as I could remember. Her talk and that diagram were nothing short of completely confusing.

"I'm glad we had this talk," my mom said, comforting me. "So now you know. O.B. doesn't mean official bazooka. They aren't toys. You'll have to find new guns for your army next time."

Utterly confused and disappointed that I had been robbed of my new weapons, I gathered up my action figures and went to the room I shared with my sister. As I set my sister's dolls on her bed, I took a long look at Barbie. She was, after all, a woman.

"Okay, Barbie," I challenged, sizing her up. "Where is your tube?"

I stripped her down and examined her body. She looked like a woman. I mean, her skin was the same color as mine. She had boobs, like my mom. She looked naked. But Barbie didn't have my line, and she didn't have that weird tube my mom told me about. This full frontal examination of a naked doll only left me more baffled.

"Screw it!" I finally conceded, throwing Barbie on the bed. "I'm never gonna bleed anyway."

*****

Three years later, I ate those words.

I was in the seventh grade when I got my first period. I was actually in *first period* when I got my first period. English. I felt this aching in my stomach, like I was hungry, even though I had eaten breakfast. Suddenly, there was this warm sensation between my legs and I felt like I had peed my pants. I looked down and saw the stain spreading across the fibers of my stone-washed jeans. I got up and ran to the bathroom; where I discovered that—despite my wanting to be a boy—I was, in fact, a girl who just got her period.

After getting cleaned up, I was sent to the nurse's office, where I was given a pair of sweat pants from the lost and found and a giant maxi pad. After a brief instruction on how to use the pad (which made more sense than my mom's tampon talk), I was sent back to class. Never mind the shroud of embarrassment that hung over me as I reentered the room wearing a new pair of pants and a foot long maxi that swooshed between my thighs like a giant diaper.

That was the beginning of my period years. I spent the next two grades wearing those hideous five dollar foot longs. I literally dreaded that time of the month each month. I swore that everyone could hear my giant maxi swooshing in the halls as I ran to class. Or squishing under me as I shifted on my seat. I even tried to hide the long, loud rip as I peeled the backing off the pad in the restroom, fearing my fellow classmates would know I was sporting something large enough to absorb Lake Michigan. And man, did those things make you saddle sore. Five days of wearing those monstrous landing strips inside your underwear felt like you just rode cross country, bareback, on a small horse.

It was one day in late summer between eighth and ninth grade, on a vacation to Florida with my best friend Allison, that I reached my maximum tolerance for the maxi pad dilemma. We had been at the beach all day, frolicking in the sand and enjoying the sun. I was on my period, wearing an ultra, giant, mile long, super absorbent pad—the equivalent of wearing Depends to the beach—under my bikini. And when we took a bathroom break, Allison suddenly discovered that she, too, was on her period.

"Jen?" she called out from her stall. "I need a dime."

"A dime? What for?"

"I just started my period."

"Okay. Stay put," I told her, as if she had any other choice. "I'll go get one."

I returned a few moments later with a dime I had borrowed from my uncle. I placed it in the slot of the coin-operated pad machine and pulled the lever. Out popped a giant cardboard box. I grabbed it and slipped it under Allison's stall door. Two minutes later, she walked out with a confused look on her face.

"Where the hell do the wings go?" she asked, looking down.

She was standing there in her cute little red bikini, with a matching ultra-absorbent maxi stuffed inside her bottoms; except hers had wings. And they were hanging down the sides of her bikini like mud flaps.

"That's it," I announced, pointing and laughing. "We're getting tampons!"

I marched back out and borrowed another twenty cents from my uncle; for soda pops, I told him. Allison and I stood in front of the tampon dispenser in the beach bathroom. The floor was wet and sandy and it smelled like piss. It wasn't the ideal spot for a first time for anything, but we were determined to become women...right there, on that day, in that bathroom.

We put our dimes in and the wall-mounted machine spit out these tiny little tampons; a welcomed reduction in size as we both stood there in our bulging bikini bottoms, hers with wings. We immediately grabbed our new pint-sized friends and ran into adjoining stalls. We put our tampons in as fast as we could and ran for the beach. But it seemed, after a few minutes in the water, that I had a problem.

Jen Ashton

"Mine keeps falling out," I told Allison, fighting the waves of the Gulf of Mexico.

"That doesn't sound right," she informed me as she shot me a horrid look. "Are you sure you put it in right?"

Another wave broke over us. "Yeah!" But the truth was, I wasn't sure at all. In fact, while in my stall I had wondered how this tiny little pad was going to replace the five dollar foot longs of my past. Though boggled, I knew that most women preferred tampons over pads. The commercials were keen in relaying that message. They were trusted by many and so why wouldn't I trust them too?

But just as the words left my mouth, I felt the tiny pad swelling bigger and bigger as it absorbed the ocean water inside my bikini. And soon enough, I was no longer trusting my tampon. "I'm gonna go back in!" I shouted across the waves. "I need to put my tampon back in!"

"I'll come with you!"

Back in the bathroom, I pulled a giant cotton blob from my bikini. I didn't understand what had gone wrong. It was then, and only then, that

Allison gave me the educational talk that my mom had tried to give me when I was ten.

"No no, no," she started. "It doesn't go between your lips. It goes *inside* them."

"Inside? What do you mean? I thought it was just a smaller pad?"

"No, it goes inside you. It's like a plug. You point it up and push it in."

"Oh!" I exclaimed, finally understanding the tube reference from my youth. "I feel so stupid. I just slid it long-ways between my lips, thinking it was a pad that you could hide in there. But it felt weird. Thank God! I was beginning to think I wasn't meant for tampons. It kept falling out!'

"And I was beginning to think you were a total slut!" Allison laughed. "Tampons only fall out of girls with huge holes!"

We borrowed another dime from a woman in the restroom and I hurried into the stall to put my new tampon in the right way. It wasn't easy, especially without training, and it made me feel funny. Nothing had ever been *inside* my body before. Nonetheless, I walked out of that stall feeling like a new woman.

Jen Ashton

"It feels funny. Does this mean I'm not a virgin anymore?" I asked.

Allison just laughed at me. But I didn't budge. I shot her a serious expression, signaling that I was serious. I really needed to know if I had just lost my virginity. That's a big deal, a mile-stone, in a young girl's life.

"Don't worry," she assured me as she opened the door to lead us back out to the beach. "You're still a virgin."

I watched her as she walked ahead of me. She was so confident, so poised. She looked like a woman now. She really knew her stuff.

"I just have one more question," I yelled, picking up speed in my steps to catch up to her. Once we were walking side by side, woman to woman, I finally asked. "How do I pee with this thing in?"

Allison giggled under her breath. "You really are silly, Jen. I swear. Yes, you can still pee with it in." She seemed amused by my ignorance, but offered her womanly wisdom once again to reassure me. "Your tampon is in your vagina. And everyone knows you pee through your butthole."

Jen Ashton

Lesson 3: It's A Girl Thing. Period

Girls Don't Poop

Jen Ashton

Lesson #4:

GROW YOUR ASSETS

I was eleven years old when I saw my first pair of tits. And by tits, I don't mean boobs. Boobs are those saggy, deflated things hanging from the women in the YMCA locker room. Tits are round, supple, voluptuous breasts, usually found on young twenty-something babes who—for lack of any other words—make you want to say *Va va voom!*

It was the summer of '87. I was eleven, ever the tomboy, and hadn't blossomed yet. My mom was still in beauty school and I was enrolled in a summer program for latchkey kids. Seems all day was too long to be home alone, so instead, I was forced to spend my days with other abandoned children. It wasn't so bad. Rather than waging battles with tampons alone, I had Ryan. Ryan was one year older than me. He was tall, cute and funny, with floppy hair and sparkly brown eyes. Soccer was his first love. And I, happened to be his second. My new boyfriend and I were inseparable from the start. You could find us at any given moment nestled up together in the tree house, trading Garbage Pail Kids and chomping on our Big League Chew. I was such a lucky girl.

Ryan's grandmother happened to live across the street from me—an apartment building reserved for the elderly—and he visited her once a month. This meant that every thirty days, I could see Ryan on a weekend, and play with him somewhere other than the playground at Kinder Care. We would run around the park, climb trees, play tag and drink lemonade on the front porch. Basically everything that kids our age did at the time. We loved to get dirty, ride bikes and climb on roofs. Especially those of the low-standing trash dumpster sheds in my neighborhood.

One fine day in the middle of summer, Ryan and I were climbing on one such roof and I fell in the dumpster. But I didn't scream. I didn't wince or gag at the smell. I didn't cry like a little girl or even get grossed out. Because rather than landing in a heap of old banana peels and used maxi pads, I had landed on a pile of magazines. Nudie ones. Looking back, I should've run home and jumped in a tub full of disinfectant—because the germs on those magazines were no doubt worse than yesterday's leftovers—but at the time, jizz wasn't a word in my vocabulary. All I knew was that I was suddenly surrounded by tits. Lots of them!

"Ryan! Get down here! I found something!" I can't imagine the look on his face when his girlfriend of two months asked him to go dumpster diving, but he didn't hesitate. We were so romantic.

"You better have a good reason for wanting me to climb into the garbage," he mumbled under his breath as he hung down from the roof.

"Just hurry," I shushed him. "I need to show you something!"

And once he joined me, I did just that. Actually, I showed him more than something. I showed him *everything*! We found ourselves sitting on what had to be someone's life-long collection of Hustler magazines. There were tits everywhere. Mountains and mountains of young, naked women with big, round tits. Their hair teased to perfection. Their lips frosted pink. And those tits! Oh my God, they were huge and so...*not* boobs! Not like any boobs I had ever seen anyway.

Ryan and I sat together for hours thumbing through that stash of nudie magazines. One after the other, hour after hour, comparing the volume and shape of each girl's *not* boobs. We were mesmerized; hypnotized even, by all the roundness and curves, areolas and nipples. By the time the sun set and I heard my mom calling me for dinner, I think we had seen more than five hundred pairs of tits. That's one thousand individual tits! That's probably more tits than I've seen in the last twenty-three years since, combined!

"What were you guys doing out there?" my mom asked when I finally turned up for dinner.

"Nothing," I lied, keeping my stash a secret.

The next morning I ran out to the dumpster to make sure my newfound smut was still there. And it sure was. One man's trash had certainly become my treasure. Every sticky page of it. I was in tit heaven and I couldn't get enough. I went to that dumpster, with or without Ryan, every day until trash day. Even on Tuesday morning when I heard the garbage truck coming around the corner to take them away, I ran as fast as I could to the dumpster shed, dove into the trash and retrieved a few of my very favorites. And just like any other sexual deviant with a secret, I hid them in a nearby carport for safe keeping.

Finally, by the end of the summer—worn by the weather and my eager little hands—my secret stash was barely even recognizable. It was time to retire my porn. But, aside from my sadness, I could

Jen Ashton

smile knowing that none of those tits had gone to waste. In one final farewell, I held the pages close to my body, rubbing the pages over the flat planes of my eleven year old chest, hoping that some of the voluptuousness would absorb into my bloodstream, and tossed them into the trash. I had a feeling those magazines got a lot more wear in my possession, than they ever did from my perverted neighbor.

*****

When school started, my mom hired a new babysitter. Her evenings were running later and later at beauty school and she needed to make sure there was someone around to make dinner for my brother and me. Enter Michele.

Michele was our neighbor. She lived in the apartment building next door with her mother, father and disgustingly sexy older brother. They all had blue eyes, bleach blonde hair and looked like they had been imported directly from Southern California. We had known their family for awhile. Michele was three years my senior and went to school with my brother. She was your typical teenager who read books on her balcony every day...until she hit puberty.

"Michele's watching you tonight," my mom said as she made me a pair of Ego waffles for breakfast.

"Cool!" I exclaimed, grabbing them from the toaster and walking out the door. I had been so immersed in my porn over the summer that I hardly remembered even seeing Michele lately. It would be good to see her.

After school that day, I walked home from the bus stop to find Michele on her balcony, doing her homework.

"Hi Michele!" I yelled up, waving my arm frantically.

"Oh. Hi, Jennie," she acknowledged. Setting her homework on the side of her lawn chair and stood up, she leaned over the railing to talk to me.

And that's when I saw them. Her tits. At some point over the summer, while I had been rubbing magazine pages on my chest and dumpster diving with my boyfriend, Michele had grown the biggest pair of tits I had ever seen on a teenager. Where the hell had those come from? As her stomach pressed against the railing, her tits hung over another foot, casting a long shadow over my pre-pubescent flatness.

Jen Ashton

"Uh," I stuttered in utter amazement. "I guess I'll see you in a bit." I forced a smile and started to walk the rest of the way home.

"I'll be over in a few," she called out to me, but all I heard was something about her humongous tits.

I ran to my room and threw myself on my bed. "Why, God? Why?" I cried. "Why can't I have huge tits too? It's not fair!"

And it wasn't fair. I had spent all summer trying to grow them. I had prayed. I had begged. I had even wished so hard for them that I swore I would never wish for anything else again if I could just grow some tits. And God had given my tits to Michele. It was so not fair!

Michele babysat me that night and for many more evenings after. She made us dinner and helped us with her homework. She wasn't very good at it, but she did try. I blamed her tits. They got in the way of her thinking. Mine too. I couldn't concentrate when they were in my face. All I could think of was how she grew them that big. It didn't help that she sat up straight and pushed them out when she was talking to you; a gesture that not only I noticed. Every boy in the neighborhood began hanging around her balcony after school. At first, there was only one or two, but after a month or so, there must've been twenty-five suitors! They all called for her, "Rapunzel, Rapunzel, show me your tits!" And sure enough, Michele would walk out onto her balcony and lean over the railing, casting a tall shadow over of each of their eager faces, and deny them one by one.

It was a sight to behold. And one that inspired me. I realized that if I wanted to get the boy's attention, I was going to have to grow a pair. A big pair. Stuffing was the cheap and immediate solution, but I didn't even have a training bra to stuff yet. I was as flat as a board and in dire need of a little help. That's when I remembered an advertisement I had read in the back of my mom's Cosmopolitan Magazine:

Breast Enlargement Cream
Increase your bust by one cup size!
Only $39.95

I ran to her room and grabbed an issue of Cosmo from her magazine rack. I flipped to the back and there it was, calling my name. All I needed now was the money. I took a deep breath and ripped the page out. Running to my room, I folded it in half and hid it in my underwear drawer for safe keeping. No one needed to know what I was up to.

And what I was up to was a genius plan to make enough money to order my breast cream. While my ad remained tucked away under my purple panties, I spent every afternoon soliciting more subscribers to my newspaper route. Day after day I knocked on doors, begging my neighbors to sign up for the Indianapolis Star.

"Good afternoon, Mr. Jones. I'm saving for my boobs. Can I count on you for your support? All you need to do is subscribe to the Sunday paper."

I delivered papers for a living, but I was becoming a salesman for a hobby. An expensive hobby at that. I knew that I would need at least ten of those jars of cream to get the tits I wanted. Unfortunately, after a month, I had only signed up four new subscribers and I hadn't even made a dent in my first jar. Damn!

Luckily, I wasn't exactly an honest child. I resorted to stealing candy bars from the local drug store and selling them to the kids at school for a 100% mark up. Surprisingly, I did pretty well as a seller of stolen goods and found myself mailing off the first order for breast cream in no time. I locked myself in my bathroom, counted my dollars, wrapped them in a blank sheet of paper with my order form, and dropped ninety-five cents in change into the envelope. After licking the stamp, I remember doing a little happy dance in front of the mirror. I was all set. Big things were coming my way. Huge.

Six weeks later, after checking the mail every single day after school, my package finally arrived.

"Jennie, something came for you in the mail," my mom announced, holding the small cardboard box in her hand. "Who is this from?" she asked under her breath, analyzing the sender's address.

"Nobody!" I snapped, snatching the box from her hands and running into the bathroom. It seemed the only safe place in the house to carry on my secret affairs.

I locked the door behind me and clawed at the cardboard packaging like a rabid beast. I was so excited to get my hands on that cream. Ripping and pulling, I finally got it open and I held the tiny jar of breast enhancing magic in my hands. This was my moment of glory, my pinnacle, the turning point of my breasthood. From this moment on, I was going to expand. In a matter of days, I was going to have deliciously supple, voluptuous breasts just like Kelly LeBrock in Weird Science.

Never mind that they would be on an eleven-year-old's body. The rest of me would catch up eventually.

I lifted my shirt and held it up under my chin. Grinning as big as I could, I opened the jar and dug my eager fingers into the cream. And--using almost all of it in one try—I globbed it on my chest and began lathering it over my little body. It took forever to rub it in. I might have used too much. I used so much of it, in fact, that I thought my hands might enlarge too. But in that moment, it didn't matter. Nothing mattered, except working that cream into my skin. If the praying didn't work, and the nudie magazine osmosis failed, I was bound and determined to make this cream succeed.

For the next several hours I couldn't keep my eyes out of my shirt. While playing with my friends, doing my homework and eating dinner, I kept peeking down my collar to see if I had any sign of growth. None. Not yet.

"Jennie, what are you doing?" my mom scolded as she scooped a spoonful of green beans on my plate. "Stop that!"

"Sorry, Mom," I apologized, but as soon as she turned away, I took another peek.

"Jennie Lynne," my father's stern voice repeated, "I think your mother just told you not to do that. Go to your room."

Those four words were music to my ears. *Go to your room.* There was nothing else in the whole world I wanted more at that moment than run to my room, lift up my shirt and examine my newly forming breasts in the mirror. So that's what I did. All night. I even fell asleep with my hands on my chest, hoping I might wake up with swollen little boobies. Thanks, Dad, your punishment was exactly what the doctor called for. Literally.

I woke up the next morning with a handful of tits. At least that's what they felt like at first. But instead of peeling down my blankets to reveal the most awesomest pair of Barbie-like bosoms, I was greeted with giant red welts and an itchy red rash caused from an allergic reaction. Not only was I having a severe reaction, but I was going to be in a shit-ton of trouble too.

Lo and behold, my mom hauled me off to the doctor's office where she told him what I had done and showed him the jar she found in my underwear drawer. I heard the two of them whispering as they examined the ingredients. I just sat there scratching my nipples and hoping they weren't going to throw away the rest of my cream. I had sold a lot of stolen candy bars to buy that stuff and I wasn't about to let any of it go to waste.

"Jennie," my doctor asked discerningly, looking at me over his bifocals, "how did you get your hands on this cream in the first place?"

Realizing if I told the truth I was going to jail for stealing, I did the next best thing. I lied and blamed it on my mom.

"From my mom's medicine cabinet," I answered softly, shooting him the most innocent face that an eleven year old, shoplifting, tit-crazed tomboy could.

Girls Don't Poop

Jen Ashton

Lesson #5:

IN CASE OF EMERGENCY

By the time I was twelve, my parents were in the middle of a grueling divorce. My brother and I were sent to live with our dad, while my sister stayed with Mom. I remember that year vividly because my dad wasn't around much to make dinner, so I primarily survived on goldfish crackers and Diet Rite. The months came and went pretty uneventfully, and before I knew it, summer was upon us again.

One such summer eve, my father graced us with two surprises. Chinese takeout, and Kimmy. Not Kim. Not Kimberly. Kimmy. Both caught me off guard. It wasn't often that our father fed us and I had no idea he had a girlfriend. I thought he and my mom were trying to work things out for the sake of us kids. I think my mom thought so too.

Kimmy was a fashion model. She was super tall—taller than my dad even—with totally eighties hair and a wardrobe to match. She had a cute little nose, a million dollar smile and static in her head. At least that's what it sounded like when she laughed. Not to mention, when she spoke. She didn't look dumb, but boy, did she sound it. Classic case of "Nice house, no furniture." And it didn't help any that she wore her hair in a ponytail ninety percent of the time, because she swung that thing around like a tassel on one of those tits from the Hustler magazines. So many times, I thought her neck was going to snap and her empty little head was going to go rolling.

It wasn't long before Kimmy had practically moved in and tried to become domesticated. It wasn't really working though. She loaded the dishwasher with Dawn, ironed holes in our clothes and even burnt our soup. She was a disaster. She looked great, but she was not gifted in the least. Case and point: when she tried to help my dad with dinner one night.

"What's for dinner, Kevin?"

"I'm making Chicken Tonight tonight, Honey."

There was a long pause, a smile, and then she opened her mouth to let out the white noise that was her laugh. I wanted to turn the channel, but before I could, she spoke. "Why are you saying tonight twice, Babe?"

My dad, less than thrilled by her inability to read the jar of chicken topping called Chicken Tonight sitting right in front of her, answered matter-of-factly. "Because, Honey, we are having Chicken Tonight…tonight."

Her pretty little forehead buckled in confusion, followed by another long moment of static. She finally hit my dad on the shoulder endearingly and said, "Kevin! Jeesh, you're still doing it. You're saying tonight twice!"

"Yes, because we're having Chicken Tonight." He assured her.

"Oh good—" she started to say, but my dad cut her off.

"Tonight."

"Honey?" Kimmy asked, looking like she was about to cry. "Are you making fun of me? I know there's not an echo in here. I can see your lips moving. I'm not that stupid."

At that point, I had had enough.

"Kim!" I shouted, walking over to the counter and picking up the jar of Chicken Tonight. "This is what we are having tonight. Look. Read it. We are having this, Chicken Tonight, tonight for dinner. Do you get it now?" I felt so relieved, but I'm not sure she did. She cried—and not because I made her feel stupid—because I called her Kim.

I knew right then and there that I'd rather be smart than pretty when I grew up. If I had to choose, I would choose brains. I never wanted a ponytail like that either. I always assumed it was pulled too tight and cut off the circulation to her brain. Or maybe it was, in all actuality, her antenna. If it was, her frequency was off. And all I knew was that I never wanted to be on that channel. If I listened to white noise all day, I would probably go dumb too.

That night-night was not the first, and it was definitely not the last, of our dilemmas with Kimmy. Dating a model hadn't exactly been all my dad thought it was cracked up to be. The fact that she was only a few years older than my brother made things kind of weird when we went out. (Most people assumed my dad had four kids, except that he was especially affectionate with one of them.) And the fact that I was smarter than Kimmy made things even weirder. My dad and my sister seemed the only ones who could get on her level; and my dad, only because he talked baby talk to her. *Oh Kimmy-wimmy Bear.*

Jen Ashton

But despite the complications, she did make it easier to win card games. Once I realized this, I often opted for family game nights, which hadn't been of any interest to me before that. So, when all was said and done, we decided to eat Chinese takeout—because it saved confusion over what was for dinner—and play cards almost every night.

One weekend while my sister was visiting, we filled up on Kung Pao Chicken and played cards until the wee hours of the night. My brother turned in first, retreating to his room in the basement. My sister and I were next. She wanted to sleep on the floor in my room, but because I didn't like her much, I made her sleep in the office. I'm assuming my dad and Kimmy headed up to his room not long after.

An hour later, I was awakened by my sister.

"Jennie," she whispered, nudging me in the arm. "Jennie, wake up. Something's wrong with Dad."

"Leave me alone," I told her, rolling over. "Go back to sleep."

My sister was only eight at the time. She was young and scared. Our dad had a long history of heart attacks spanning the previous decade. He was unusually young to have so many and it alarmed our whole family. He was on nitrates and a shitload of other medications, but we were all still a little frightened that another cardiac arrest could hit at any given moment. So when my sister was startled in the middle of the night by noises coming from his bedroom, she immediately got up and tried to wake me.

"But Jennie," she whined.

"Go away!" I moaned.

I wasn't budging. My sister grew more worried by the minute, and rather than call 911, she called our mom.

"Mom," she cried. "Something's wrong with Dad."

"Is he okay? What happened?"

"I don't know," she wimpered. "Kimmy's in his room yelling, *Oh, God! Oh God, Kevin!* over and over again. I think Dad's dying. I don't know what to do!"

It was at this moment that my mother found out that she and my father were not, in fact,

Jen Ashton

reconciling, and that he was sleeping with Kimmy. I have no idea how she kept it together on the phone enough to instruct my sister further.

"Your dad's not dying, Sweetie. Go sleep in Jennie's room," my mom told her. "And shut the door."

"I tried. She won't let me."

"Then go downstairs and sleep in your brother's room."

"But Dad's dying! I think he's having another heart attack. Kimmy's yelling at him. Listen!"

My sister stretched the phone cord down the hall and held the phone up to my dad's bedroom door. It must have taken every ounce of strength in my mother's body at that moment not to reach through the phone and strangle her own daughter.

"Oh God! Oh God! Oh, Kevin! Oh God!"

My mom's eyes rolled through the phone and she probably reminded herself to roll over in her grave after she died too.

"I'm scared, Mom. I think I should call 911." my sister cried.

"No!!! Don't do that!" my mom shouted.

"The door's locked, Mom. I don't know what to do. Kimmy needs help! I'm gonna knock so she'll let me in."

"No, no, no! Don't do that!" my mom interjected. "Leave them alone. Just go downstairs and sleep in your brother's room.

"Okay," she finally agreed, dragging the phone back to the office. After she hung up, my sister went downstairs and woke up our brother. "Brian, Dad's dying and Jennie won't wake up."

"What? Who's dying?" my brother was confused and groggy. "What are you talking about?

"Kimmy's yelling at Dad because he's dying and Jennie won't get up. I called Mom and she said to sleep in your room."

"What's wrong with Dad?"

"I don't know. The door's locked and Kimmy keeps yelling, *Oh God, Kevin! Oh God!* I think he's having another heart attack."

My brother was old enough to know what was going on. "And you called *Mom*?!!!"

"Yeah, she told me to come sleep down here with you."

"Why not Jennie's room?

"Jennie hates me. There's no way she's gonna let me sleep with her. Mom said to sleep in your room."

"Well, you can't sleep in here," he informed her. "C'mon," he said, dragging her back upstairs, "you're sleeping in Jennie's room whether she likes it or not."

My brother led my sister up two flights of stairs, doing their best to be quiet as they passed our father's bedroom. When they entered my room, I was already awake.

"Jen?" my brother's voice strained. "Are you up?"

"She's not sleeping in here."

"Shhh. Yes she is. Don't wake Dad. Just let her sleep on the floor. Just tonight. We'll figure this all out in the morning."

"Nope! Not gonna happen."

"I need you to calm down," my brother encouraged, "just let her stay in here. She's scared."

"I don't give a shit!" I yelled. I was not really a morning person; especially a two o'clock in the morning person. "Get out!!!"

My mother always told me that I talked too loud. And sure enough, that night, I talked way too loud. Suddenly, we heard footsteps--heavy, stomping footsteps—and then we heard a doorknob turning, and a lock clicking. After that, we heard the deep groan of our father's voice. The light in the hallway turned on and I saw his shadow coming toward my room.

"Oh shit! Hide!" I shouted. We all hid under my covers.

"What the hell is going on in here?" my dad shouted back, turning on the light in my bedroom. We were all hiding on my bed, a giant mound of bodies trying their best not to be seen, breathe or laugh. I was half-frightened and half-hysterical. "I said, what are you guys doing in here?" he repeated as he pulled back the covers to reveal all

Jen Ashton

three of his children pretending to be asleep. But my sister immediately broke from character.

"Daddy! You're alive!" she cried out, jumping up and hugging his leg.

I looked up to find my dad wearing a pair of bicycle shorts, his hair a mess and flushed cheeks. "More like, what are *you* doing?' I offered with a side of sarcasm. Kimmy walked up behind him with the same wild hair and flushed cheeks. She was wearing a robe.

"We were doing what adults do." It was the only explanation my brother needed. He rose from his faux-sleep and walked past both of them without saying a word.

"What do you mean, Daddy?" my sister asked, and that set the tone for my first would-be sex talk.

"Well, pumpkin, you see…uh…when two people love each other—"

"So you love Kimmy, Dad?"

My dad shot Kimmy a look and answered hesitantly. "Well, yes, in certain ways. I guess I do."

"What about Mom?" she asked. Her innocent question sent Kimmy back to our dad's bedroom. Quickly.

That was my breaking point too. I had heard enough. You never want to hear about your parents having sex. But what's worse, is hearing about your parents having sex with other people. Or *hearing* them have sex with other people, for that matter. I didn't know exactly what was happening in that bedroom, but I was perfectly fine with never hearing about it. The most important thing was that my dad wasn't dead. I didn't care about anything else, except sleep. So as he and my sister sat down on my bed to have a talk about the birds and the bees, I grabbed my pillow and headed for the office, walking out on my one and only chance for a bit of formal sex education.

Lesson #6:

THE IMPORTANCE OF BROWNIE POINTS

I was in the sixth grade the first time I felt someone else's tongue in my mouth and it scared me to death. I had been kissing boys for years before that. A peck here, a kiss there. But never with tongue, and always behind closed doors. Or curtains, as was the case with my very first boyfriend, David.

David was my first love. I was five years old. We were neighbors and we played from sun-up until the street lights came on, every single day. I can't remember the exact day we became an item, but before we knew it, we were kissing every chance we got. The only problem was finding a place to do it. After a few failed attempts in an old tractor tire that smelled like piss, I suggested the next best place: my bathroom. It wasn't a far hike and the ripe stench of urine was a bit more subtle. He agreed.

Jen Ashton

"Close the door," I ordered him. We didn't have locks back then, so I pulled out a cabinet drawer to prevent anyone from coming in. "Now get in the shower."

David and I both stepped into the shower and pulled the shower curtain closed. Certain that we had enough privacy, we closed our eyes and counted.

"One, two, three!" On three, we both leaned in and planted a kiss on the other's lips. It was so romantic. (Albeit, the first thousand tries left us with purple knots on our foreheads.) It would be awhile before we mastered any kind of gentle restraint.

David and I kissed for years. Every day, after school, before snack, after dinner, you name it, we were kissing prior to, or post it. And every day it was the same routine. Run upstairs. Close the door. Open the drawer. Get in the shower. Close the curtain. Close our eyes. Count to three. Kiss! All just to make sure no one saw us. We were sure what we were doing was wrong. We were naughty…deviant…sinners.

I eventually moved away and had to find a new boy to kiss behind the shower curtain each day. And needless to say, there were plenty of takers. I pecked my way up the ranks. By the sixth grade, I had earned myself quite the reputation as a slut. I was the bad girl. The girl who lured innocent boys to the deaths of their virgin lips. I was a thief and proud of it; until one memorable day when *my* mouth was de-virginized by my brand new boyfriend of two hours named Blue-eyed Mike.

*****

I was playing kickball on a patch of grass in the parking lot across from our house—appropriately called the island—when I first saw his bright blue eyes. Mike. Mike was my age, except puberty had been kind to him. He was tall and tan with the most beautiful blue eyes I had ever seen. To offset the balance of his face, he also happened to possess the most succulent lips our side of the equator. Man, were they big. Women nowadays pay thousands of dollars to have lips like that. He was a freak of nature.

But freak or not, Mike was hot. With his raspy voice—deeper than the other boys—and a smile that melted even the coldest of winter days, I knew from the first time I met him that I was going to make him mine.

"Mind if I join?" Mike asked, shooting me that million-dollar smile.

"If you can keep up," I snapped, kicking him the ball. "You know how to play?"

"I kick the ball, right?" he joked.

I liked his attitude, so I offered him a spot on my team.

It was cold that day. Either late fall or early winter. The ground was frozen under our feet. I was wearing my signature pegged jeans, turtleneck, cleats and windbreaker. (Most likely my dad's. I always raided his closet. Those biker shorts from the Kimmy incident? They became my favorite article of clothing when I was a teenager. They didn't exactly cling to my thighs like they were supposed to—and I didn't necessarily ride bikes in them either—but I rocked them just the same.)

Blowing warm air on my hands to keep my fingers from going numb, I ran to my position on the field. Mike joined me. "You live around here?" I asked, jogging backward to talk to him.

"Just moved in," he informed me. "That building over there." He pointed to an apartment building adjacent to mine.

Lesson 6: The Importance of Brownie Points

"Cool. Welcome to the neighborhood," I huffed. But welcome to my *life* was more like it. I tried not to stare. He was just so sexy, wearing his navy sweater and black gloves. He looked warm, but his nose and cheeks were growing increasingly red as the wind nipped his face. "Cold out here, huh?"

"Yeah."

"Want some hot cocoa?"

"You got marshmallows?"

"Maybe," I flirted.

"The small kind?"

"I can check."

And that's all it took. He shot me that hundred-watt smile and I held my hands up in the form of a T. "Time!" I called to the other players. "We're heading in. See you assholes tomorrow!" I was such a lady.

Mike followed me to my house. We walked in, took off our shoes and headed straight for the floor vent in the living room. Peeling off his gloves, he sat next to me where we roasted our hands like hogs on a spit, turning occasionally.

"So what's your name?" he asked.

"Jennie."

"I'm Mike."

"Cool."

Our conversation was about as deep as a puddle. It wasn't that I didn't want to talk to talk to him, I just didn't know *how* to. It was the first time a boy had ever made me nervous. I looked into the deep blue seas of his eyes and I got the warm tingle. And it just took over. I didn't know what to do. He made me smile. He made me feel girly. He made me want to kiss those big, pillowy pink lips. They were staring me in the face. I could feel their magnetism drawing me closer. And closer. I was mere inches from kissing him. I could feel his warm breath on my frozen face. My lips were stretching to reach his.

"So you go to Carmel?" he interrupted.

I pulled my lips back into my own face, "Uh—yeah—sixth grade. You?"

Jen Ashton

Now kiss me you fool!

"Sixth."

"Cool." I realized I wasn't getting anywhere, so I stood up and offered him some hot cocoa.

*****

Mike and I sat on two bar stools at the kitchen counter sipping our Swiss Miss and chewing our freeze-dried marshmallows. Slurping and smiling, we played footsie and tested each other's boundaries. His socks rubbed against my socks. I returned the favor. And within five minutes, he was my boyfriend.

With that out of the way, it was easy to make the next move.

"You wanna go to the shower and kiss?"

"The *what* to do *what*?"

"The shower. You want to kiss me in there?"

"I was actually thinking we could just hang out for awhile first."

"Really???" I was shocked. His lips had been calling my name for a whole ten minutes already. "What did you want to do?"

"I don't know. Wanna go for a walk?"

A walk? I wanted to feel those soft, billowing pink mounds on his face pressed against mine. I wanted to close my eyes and count to three. I wanted to accidently knock foreheads as we moved in for our first kiss. And he wanted to go on a walk. Wow. He must be one of those boys who liked me for my personality that my mom told me about. I guess I was just going to have to use it then. Yep. I would be using my personality to persuade Mike into our first kiss.

Mike and I held hands as we strolled around the island for an hour. By the time we came in, I think I had a mild case of frostbite on my ass. The bitter cold had convinced us to return to our floor vent, but by then, my mom was home so we opted for the laundry room in my apartment building. It was private, inside, and most importantly, warm.

"Sit up here," Mike suggested, hoisting me up onto the dryer.

One of the residents was doing laundry and the heat emanating from the coin-operated machine was enough to defrost my bottom. Mike scooted in close, unzipping my windbreaker. He had a hungry look in his eyes that I immediately mirrored back. I had never kissed a boy in the laundry room before and I wasn't sure how romantic it felt. The washer was spinning. The dryer was shaking underneath me. Someone's zipper was methodically clinking against the inside of one of them. It was loud. Definitely not the kind of scene the Maytag man would be proud of. But Mike leaned in and kissed me anyway.

It started out like every other kiss, except his was softer. I swore he was storing a few of those marshmallows in his lips. But instead of pulling away after the initial peck, Mike reached up and held my face with his cold-ass hands.

"Brrr..." I managed to say. "Your hands are—"

And that's when it happened. In the middle of my sentence—while my mouth was wide open—Mike slipped his tongue inside my mouth.

"Bleh!" I screamed, spitting his tongue out of my mouth. "Gross! What *was* that?"

He tried to move in for seconds, but I was having none of that. What had he just done? Why did he lick my tongue? I saw a guy do something like that in a movie once. His wife was eating a brownie and he decided he wanted some, so he ate it out of her mouth. At least that's what my mom told me.

"Just kiss me," Mike whispered, holding his lips close to mine. This would've been the moment I was waiting for; the one I had been hoping for when we were roasting our fingers; the one I fantasized about for a whole five minutes over Swiss Miss and our sock seduction. But, it was ruined now.

"No way! That was sick. I almost puked." I pushed him away and hopped down. "I never want to see you again, Mike! We're breaking up." I shoved my finger in my mouth and simulated a gagging reflex, opened the door of the laundry room and stomped out.

I ran inside my house, straight past my mom to my bedroom where I threw myself on the bed. I was too grossed out to eat dinner. There was absolutely nothing sexy about Blue-eyed Mike anymore. In fact, his eyes looked more grey than blue. His lips were soft, sure, I would give him that, but he needed to keep them shut. The fact that he didn't, meant that I had just been violated by his wandering tongue. A slippery slope I wasn't prepared to venture down yet. He took my French-kiss virginity. That asshole.

"Jennie?" my mom called, knocking on my bedroom door. "Dinner's ready."

"I'm not hungry," I yelled from underneath my pillow. I was hiding my shame.

"It's pork chops," she tempted.

"I don't care."

"I have A-1," she persuaded.

"I don't care!"

"But you love pork chops, honey. Is something wrong?"

"No! Just leave me alone."

Never one to listen, my mom sat down next to me and scratched my back. "Did that boy hurt your feelings?"

"What boy?"

"The one I saw you walking with outside earlier. Did you guy's break up?"

"I don't know. I think so. I pushed him."

"Why?"

"Because he tried to steal a brownie out of my mouth and I wasn't even *eating* a brownie!"

"He what?"

"Never mind, Mom. You wouldn't understand. Just go away. Please."

I spent the rest of the evening in my room trying to process the events that took place that day. Tossing and turning, I replayed that disgusting moment over and over again inside my head. The more I thought about it, the more I wanted to call him up and tell him just how mad I was. *Mike, your tongue was so slimy! Do you have any idea how gross that felt?* I finally decided to get up and wash my mouth out with Plax. At least then I could sleep knowing I hadn't gotten any of his kooties.

*****

I ran into Mike at the bus stop the following Monday morning. I didn't even look at him. How could I? He had violated my mouth with his— his—his soft, velvety tongue. Wait a minute*?* Why was I suddenly turned on by the memory of his French kiss; a kiss that almost made me gag? I was convinced that he was disgusting. But as I stood there thinking of how sweet he tasted, his delicate lips and moist kiss, I had a revelation. *Oh my God. I think I'm in love with him.*

As we shuffled onto the bus that morning, I pledged that I was going to get Mike back. As gross as that invisible brownie-stealing kiss had been, I wanted another one. There was something about it that was calling me back for a second try, another taste. Maybe I had misjudged it. Maybe it wasn't so sick after all. Maybe that feeling of wanting to puke was actually just butterflies in my stomach churning with pre-teen sexual excitement. Whatever it was, I wanted it back. Besides, Mike had de-virginized my tongue. That meant we *had* to be together. I might even have to marry him.

But try as I may, week after week, month after month, Mike never took me back. My words had been too harsh, my reaction too offensive. Perhaps I had been too immature about the whole thing. After all, I *was* twelve and a half. I was almost a teenager and growing up fast. If I wanted people to take me seriously as an adult, I was going to have to swallow a few tongues. Hopefully, without puking.

Girls Don't Poop

Jen Ashton

Lesson #7:

I MIGHT BE GOING TO HELL

By the time I was ready for a formal education about sex, there was no one around to teach me. I was thirteen, curious and already practicing on my Donnie Wahlberg pillow. He gave me the warm tingle. So, like any other hot-blooded American girl, I had his face plastered on everything I owned. Donnie Wahlberg posters. Donnie Wahlberg lunchbox. Donnie Wahlberg bed sheets. And my favorite, an almost life-size Donnie Wahlberg body pillow.

Easy to hug and easy to hump, my Donnie pillow and I were going steady. Three nights a week. I had to give my little hoohah a break between dates because the pillowcase wasn't exactly 1200 thread count. Nevertheless, we were an item. Every other night, I would play my New Kids On the Block cassette tape while Donnie sang to me. He showered me with compliments. *Jen,*

Jen Ashton   107

you've got the right stuff. I love the way you turn me on. His sweet nothings were music to my ears. I stared him down with my thirteen-year-old seduction and jumped his bones—or cotton fibers—in one single bound!

"Oh, Donnie! I love the way you sing to me. *Muah, muah, muah*—" I swooned as I wrapped my arms around him and devoured him with wet kisses. It was like this for us every night we were together. He never resisted. Donnie "body pillow" Wahlberg was the best boyfriend a girl could have. Except that he wasn't real.

One night while we were gettin' our horizontal-tango on in the top bunk of my bunk bed, I realized that my soft moans were being echoed by that of another. But when I took a break from showing Donnie just how Rico Suave I could be under the sheets, I was met with silence.

"Who the hell was that?" I asked aloud, looking down at Donnie's face. "How dare they interrupt!" My hair all a mess, my hormones quivering inside my polka-dotted panties, I was thoroughly dismayed by the sheer nerve of someone interrupting our alone time. But gazing back down at Donnie's permanent smile, I quickly returned to the throes of love-making. "Never mind them," I assured him. "Let's get back to business!" And with my best sexy-voice, I imitated a cat's meow just before I pounced on his delicious, rectangular, cotton-filled body.

"*Oh! Oh! Oh!*" I heard again. This time closer and more clear. "*Yes! Right there! Oh yes!*"

I pulled the sheets off my head and looked around. There wasn't supposed to be anyone home. It was a school night. My brother worked late at Little Caesar's and my dad was out with Kimmy. My brother was borderline gay at the time, and those coos, were definitely not coming from my dad's girlfriend. I knew the sound of her sexual expressions by now. These new noises...they were different. They were more like animalistic grunts. *Uh, uh uh!!! Oh yeah! Ooooooh yeah!*

That's when it donned on me. Despite the deafening octave, that particular sex wasn't close by. It was down in our basement. Yep. Voices carry—right through the vents. Those angelic sounds of pleasure were escaping the lips of my housekeeper, Marla.

Marla was a portly woman in her mid-twenties. I think she used to work in my dad's office, but she lost her job. The story gets a bit muddled from there. Some say, broke and homeless, she cried and cried and cried, so much so that my dad felt sorry for and offered her to take up residency in our basement in return for "light housekeeping." Others—me—say my dad was probably porking her. Keep your friends close, and your secretaries closer.

I listened a little longer. The verbiage was more like instruction and praise. Kimmy had been more into random bursts of religious exclamations. But Marla, she told her man exactly what she wanted and how she wanted it. *"Oh yes! Put it right there. Yeah!!! Don't move. Spank me. Harder. That's good! Now turn over. Yes! Hold my legs."*

My thirteen-year-old brain couldn't conceive of what was actually happening down there, but it sure did sound like a good time. Something about listening to Marla moan like that not only made me feel like an eavesdropper, but it also made me feel very, very naughty. It gave me the warm tingle. And there was only one thing to do with it—take it out on Donnie.

"Come here you sexy hunk of a man-pillow! I'm gonna ravage you!"

And just like that, I threw the sheets back over our heads and went to town; this time, trying a few new moves. *Oh yes, Donnie! Right there. Here, let*

Jen Ashton

me prop my legs up on you. Good. Ok, now turn over, I'm going to spank you.

*****

The next day I ran into Marla after school. She was cleaning the half bath in our foyer when I walked through the front door.

"Oh. Hey, Marla," I said, greeting her as I lobbed my backpack into the God-awful Papasan chair my dad insisted was an early nineties status quo.

"Hi, Jennie," she replied, looking over her shoulder at me.

She stood there swirling the toilet brush around the bowl as I stared her down. I didn't mean to stare. (Yes I did.) I was just curious. I wondered who was down in the basement with her last night and what spanking had to do with lying on top of her. (At that time, that's all I thought sex was. Two people who love each other, the man lying on top of the woman. And, in my case with Donnie, maybe a little dry-humping, because it felt good on my hoohah.)

"What's up?" Marla interrupted.

"Oh, nothing," I answered, swaying back and forth in my flannel shirt, pegged jeans and boat shoes.

"That's an awful big smirk on your face for nothing" she retorted, flushing the toilet and turning toward me. "Is there something on your mind?"

"Well—uh—kinda," I conceded. "I wanted to ask you something."

"Sure. Ask me anything."

That was the first time someone had ever offered up such freedom. The freedom to ask anything. Wow, that was such a huge and overwhelming proposal. Why was the sky blue? Why didn't they show the octopus on the theater version of Goonies? Why hadn't George Lucas made Star Wars IV yet? Oh wait! Or had he? Those were the big questions. But not the ones lingering on the forefront of my mind as I gazed upon Marla's large backend; one that should've required a sticker on her back pocket that warned other pedestrians of her "wide load."

It didn't seem appropriate though, to just come right out and ask about the spanking thing. So I resorted to something a little less obvious. "I heard you having sex last night."

Marla's face turned whiter than her already pale complexion. In fact, I think I saw all the color in her cheeks wash right down the toilet with the blue cleanser, creating a purple swirl of shame and embarrassment.

"I wanted to ask you about it."

The color returned to her face. "About what exactly?"

"Sex."

"My sex? Or just sex in general."

"Just sex in general."

A hint of relief filled her lungs as she followed it with a deep sigh. She looked around to make sure no one else was home and then motioned to the basement with her eyes.

"Follow me," she instructed—she was good at instruction from what I could tell so far—and grabbed her cleaning supplies. "We should probably talk in my room."

I followed Marla down to the basement where she invited me into her room. There wasn't much to it. Just a bed—a bouncy one from what I heard last night—and a dresser. She set her cleaning supplies on the floor and peeled the giant yellow gloves from her hands before she sat down.

"Come sit," she motioned, patting her hand on the foot of the bed next to where she sat. "Let's talk."

I reluctantly took a seat, despite my inner excitability. Part of me was so nervous and gitty to finally hear about all the goings-on under the covers. But another part of me was petrified of losing my innocence forever. What if it's gross? What if sex is this disgusting thing I'm going to have to do with a boy if I love him? Does it hurt? It sure sounds like it does. All those grunts and moans. It sounds like my friend Allison when she broke her arm. *Oooooh! Oh God! Oh God!* I had to know more.

"What's sex like?" I asked bluntly.

"Sex? Well—uh—it's magical. It's what two people do when they love each other."

"So who was the guy you had sex with then?"

"My boyfriend."

"And you love him?"

"Yes."

"Were you in trouble?"

Her brow buckled. "In trouble? For what?"

"I don't know. He was spanking you. Did you do something bad?"

Marla laughed under her breath and her color faded again. There was a long pause before she found the right words to explain her sadomasochism to me. "No, no, no," she giggled. "I didn't do anything bad. It's hard to explain to a thirteen year old, but sometimes—sometimes people do things in the bedroom that sound like they are bad, but they are actually good."

"I'm not following you."

"Okay," she sighed, settling in for a long talk, "let me just shoot it to you straight. Spanking is bad when you are little. Your parents spank you because you need to be punished—"

I nodded my head. I understood that part. I had been spanked by my parents with a wooden spoon all my life. I had even been spanked by my principal once. In the first grade I was suddenly overcome by the overwhelming desire to stand up and shout out every single curse word I owned in my seven-year-old vocabulary. *Shit! God Damn! Fuck! Bastard! Asshole! Dammit to Hell! Shit! Fuck you!* I ran out of that classroom as fast as I could and hid in the coat closet down the hall. Better believe that when the teacher found me, I was sent straight to the office to be punished for my momentary Tourette's.

"But when you're older—well, things are different." Marla continued. "Spanking feels good."

"It does?"

"Well, yes. Sometimes. I guess it depends on the situation. But when someone you love is doing it, it can feel good."

I didn't get it. My mom loved me. My dad loved me. And it still felt bad when they spanked me. But whatever. Next.

"So where does he put his thingy?" I wanted to get straight to the details. I had seen enough pseudo-porn on Cinemax to know that boy's *thingies* got bigger as they got older. So naturally, I figured it would get in the way when he had to lay down on top of her.

"It goes inside."

"Inside *where*?!!!" My question was innocent enough. Up until that time, the only thing I was aware of putting inside my body was a tampon.

Marla spent the next hour explaining sex to me. Detail for detail. From what feels good to what doesn't. From positions to penis size, copping a feel to copulation. This sex stuff was sounding fantastic!

"...and that's how you get pregnant," she concluded.

Complete silence on my end. Marla had just squashed all my teenage fantasies and sexual desires with that statement. There was no way I was getting pregnant. Nuh-uh. Nope. No way. My mother would kill me.

"But I'll tell you little secret," she whispered graciously. "If you do anal—" she paused as she placed her hand over her top lip, "you *can't* get pregnant!"

I had no idea what anal was, but by the smile on Marla's face, I knew it was good. It had to be. You could do it and not get pregnant! Yep! Anal was right up my alley. I was so thankful for my talk with Marla that day. Her wisdom was music to my ears—even sweeter than The New Kid's singing *Please Don't Go Girl*.

"And besides," she offered as last words, "it feels better."

Better than the warm tingle? *And* my mom won't kill me? I was sold.

*****

The next day I waltzed into school feeling like a new woman. Not only was I completely knowledgeable in the sexual education department now, but I was also the brand new proprietor of a super saucy trade secret. One I couldn't wait to share...with anyone and everyone.

My first opportunity to boast of my newfound knowledge came as I made my way to first period. I walked past a group of fellow seventh grade girls talking about sex before the bell. And without an invitation into their conversation, I offered up my opinion.

Jen Ashton

"When I do it, I'm doing anal. You can't get pregnant that way." I said this very matter-of-factly as I stood up straight and proud, puffing out my chest under my neon-colored sweater. Turning my nose up at them, I strutted away like the queen of information. Three down.

Next was a group of girls I knew. We were working in a study group in English class, second period.

"Hey," I whispered, "are you guys still virgins?" Everyone nodded yes. "Good, because my housekeeper told me a secret about sex. She said if you do anal, you can't get pregnant. I know that's what *I'm* going to be doing once I lose my virginity. Do you know how much trouble I would be in if I got pregnant?" Four more down.

I didn't stop there. By mid day I had told about a hundred other students about my plans to do anal. I was so mature, so wise. I had all the knowledge. I was a wealth of information. Anal was the secret to my success. Watch out, Michael J. Fox!

"Have you guys done anal?" I asked of two eighth graders standing near the water fountain. "It's all the rage."

"I heard you're not a virgin anymore," I snapped at a girl named Jill. Her locker was five down from mine and I had witnessed the multitude of ninth grade boys frequenting her. Rumor had it she was sleeping with all of them. That whore. "Well, I wouldn't want you to get pregnant," I told her. "I would do anal if I were you. Beats not knowing who the dad is."

At lunch, I overheard a few girls in the restroom talking about sex. They were giggling and laughing, talking about this guy and that guy as they applied their frosted lip gloss. I flushed the toilet and stepped out of the stall wearing my dad's neon cable-knit sweater, pegged jeans and hiking boots. They all looked up at me through the reflection in the mirror. I put my hand on my chest and gasped as if I was disgusted with their conversation. After a dramatic huff and puff, I again offered up my opinion.

"Yuck! I can't believe you guys are having regular sex. Everyone knows that anal is the new thing. You can't get pregnant. Duh." And then I left them to consider my condescension as I headed to the lunchroom. It was pizza day.

As I sat down and opened my carton of chocolate milk and planned to dive into my hexagon-shaped pizza, I was quickly scooped up by the vice principal.

"Jennie," he ordered, "I need you to come with me." I began gathering my plastic ware and milk, but he interjected. "You can leave those here. You won't be returning to lunch."

Oh boy, I was in trouble. I wondered if it was because I had put gum under my desk in Mrs. White's history class. Or if it was in regards to me cursing at my gym teacher when I didn't want to do calisthenics. Maybe Mrs. Hodgkins had finally discovered who stole all the test answers from her office. Whatever it was, it was bad enough that I was being hauled off by my collar in front of everyone.

"Jennifer," the principal formerly addressed me once I arrived in his office, "we seem to have a problem. Some of your teachers have grown concerned over something they've heard today. I've been informed that you have been talking to many students about sex. Specifically, a certain kind of sex."

I sunk down in my seat. If he knew my secret, he would tell me mom. She would find out my plan to have sex. Or worse, my plan to do anal so I could hide it from her.

"It is very important that you understand something, young lady. We do not discuss these kinds of things on school property—or anywhere—for that matter. You should be ashamed of yourself. What you speak of is disgusting and shameful. It is reserved for deviants, monkeys and boys who like boys. This kind of behavior serves no purpose other than to put you on a fast track to Hell, where you will be bound to eternal damnation for your actions and burn there forever."

At the time, I thought this was his way of scaring me into wanting children. I had no idea, until I got home that evening, what the actual definition of anal sex was and why I had been scorned so harshly. It would still be a year or two before I would fully grasp the concept. When you're thirteen, a hole is a hole, and losing your virginity is going to hurt any way you look at it. (Although, somewhere in the back of my head was the memory of Marla's smile. Maybe she *did* know what she was talking about. She was having sex, after all. Lots of it, from what I gathered in our conversation. And she made it sound so good.)

Either way, at the end of that day, I was grounded for a month and put on birth control. My bubble had been burst and I was dead set on never

Jen Ashton

doing anal. *Unless*—I told myself—I somehow found that I was already guaranteed an eternal seat in hell for *something else* I did along the way. Then—and only then—I just might have to reconsider following Marla's sage advice and partake in the sinful pleasures of gays and monkeys.

Girls Don't Poop

Lesson #8:

WATCH YOUR MOUTH

Just in case my trip to the principal's office hadn't taught me to watch my mouth, life made sure I got a second chance to get it right. And what better way to drive home a lesson than to enlist a little help from my friends.

Jill was my fun, fat friend who was the life of every teenage house party. BYOB: Bring Your Own Boobs. Don't get me wrong, she brought booze too, but her boobs made more of a statement than a fifth of Jim Beam.

"Look out, boys!" she warned upon entrance, taking off her top. "Simon and Garfunkel are here!" She loved flaunting her gargantuan duo in the faces of lesser equipped ninth graders. She was loud, funny and unapologetic. Her personality was larger than life and she had the body to match. You could say she was *well-rounded*. She also had one other sizeable attribute she didn't mind exposing to the other students. Her mouth. And she wasn't shy about having a party in there either.

Jill was crowned Queen of the Blowjobs in the summer of '91. I have no recollection of who actually crowned her, the ceremony or if she was, in fact, even given a tiara, but I do remember how she earned her title. Looking back, I'm still not sure if it was a goal she set out to accomplish on her own, or if she was just gratuitously given her name by her many fans. It could be, that she just really liked pleasing teenage boys.

Jill had a monopoly on our entire class. Save none for me. The boys I crushed on weren't nearly as interested in me as they were Jill's Saturday Lip Service. Yep, you heard that correctly. She had her own program. Just like clockwork, or—for lack of a better description—church, Jill held services every Saturday in the pine bush at the end of her driveway. Every hour on the hour. No boy was exempt. Anyone could schedule an appointment.

I routinely stayed over at Jill's on Friday nights. Not because I wanted to witness her hourly sessions, but because there was a boy named Chris that I liked who lived across the golf course from her. He was only one of a few who hadn't been to Jill's Saturday service—mainly because he was going steady with a girl named Lisa—so my odds

Jen Ashton

were good that he was actually sneaking over to see me, and not Jill's mouth. Chris and I would meet on Friday nights—after Jill's parents went to bed—so we could make out. I would let him get to first or second base and then I would chicken out and send him home. Every single weekend. Still, he came back for more. One Friday, we went to third and I punched him. I was never very good at responding to new experiences.

The next morning, I sat on the couch with Jill watching Ricki Lake reruns.

"Oh no he didn't!" one guest yelled on TV. Her nephew walked out on stage dressed like a woman in a push-up bra and tube top. The audience roared in a frenzy of boos and cheers.

"Oh yes he did!" we shouted back, throwing cheeseballs at the screen.

Life as we knew it was normal. Just a typical Saturday morning in the suburbs. That was…until I caught something out of the corner of my eye. I peered through the big bay window of Jill's living room to witness the arrival of her first appointment that day. The boy rode his bike slowly, looking around suspiciously as he approached the bush in the front yard. He quickly dumped his bike by the mailbox and crawled into Jill's burning bush of love.

"Welp," she said, rotating her jaw in a circular motion and stretching her lips, "time to go. Brandon's here."

While her dad mowed the lawn in the backyard and her mom made a fresh boysenberry pie in the kitchen, Jill walked down her long driveway, looking both ways for any sign of neighborly traffic in the adjacent yards. Certain the coast was clear, she quietly climbed under the evergreen foliage and slipped into her blowjob lair of guilty pleasures: servicing the neighborhood boys since 1989.

As I watched her disappear, I found it funny that no one seemed to find it strange that a new bike lay at the base of her mailbox every hour of each Saturday. And no one found it peculiar that Jill frequently went to "check the mail." It's not like she was expecting her breast cream order to arrive. She was already blessed with more tit per square inch then all the girls in Hustler combined. Stranger still, no one even seemed to notice the disappearing boys, or that Jill crawled in and out of that bush, or that the bush provided a heavenly haven beyond its needles and neatly trimmed landscaping.

Jen Ashton

But I did.

The minutes ticked away like hours as I sat on the edge of my seat. Each sixty-second stretch dragged longer and longer. I curiously wondered what was happening inside that bush. I wasn't even sure what a blowjob was. I knew it had something to do with blowing and something to do with boys. Clearly, my young mind was unable to stretch as far as Jill's lips. Ten minutes after the mysterious disappearance of Brandon, Jill crawled out of one side of the bush, wiping her mouth, while Brandon darted out the other side like a rabbit. He jumped on his bike and rode away. Smiling.

One down, six more to go. Jill's service wouldn't technically end until dinnertime. Until then, she returned to the house, where we proceeded to watch our talk shows between appointments. It amazed me just how many boys faithfully returned week after week. One by one they arrived, and left with a smile. And not just average boys, the hot ones too! I watched in teenage awe as the hours passed and the boys *came* and went. There had to be something to these blowjob things and I wanted in on it. So like any young Padawan, I solicited the wise counsel of my Blowjob Jedi master.

"Teach me," I insisted, greeting her at the door as she returned from her last session that evening.

"I can't."

"Teach me," I repeated, buckling my brow and placing my hands on my hips. It was my own mind trick. I wasn't moving and there was no way she was getting through my invisible force field.

"I can't, Jen. It's the code."

"The code? What code?"

"The fat girl code."

"What the hell is that?"

She sighed, reluctantly revealing her secret. "Big girls need an advantage over you skinny-minnies. Blow jobs are that advantage."

"Please???" I shot her my best puppy dog eyes. I had been practicing them ever since I bought my first Pound Puppy when I was seven. But Jill wasn't budging.

I needed to think fast. I wanted in on this fat girl code. If I had to eat ten thousand peanut butter sandwiches to become a fat girl, I was going to do

Jen Ashton

it. It wasn't fair. My rail-thin body was genetic. Why did my mom have to be so skinny? If she was fat, I would be a Blowjob Jedi by now. Even if she was big-boned, I'd have a foot in the door.

"I just want to try one on Chris. I won't take any of your boys. Promise. Just show me. Please?"

*****

That night, Jill and I found the privacy we needed for our Jedi training in her attic, complete with a swamp…cooler.

"Okay," she began, "hold your Coke bottle like this. And put your mouth on it like this."

I mirrored her with my own bottle. And then I watched as she did unspeakable things to that poor, innocent Coke bottle—of which had absolutely *nothing* to do with blowing.

"And then you—uh hem—sorry, I think I have a frog in my throat." It wasn't the first slimy thing she had in her throat that day. "Uh hem," she coughed again, "Can you give me a minute? I'll be right back."

She left me alone in the attic while she went downstairs and rinsed her mouth out with mouthwash. Something she should've done after every appointment. Once alone with my makeshift penis, I got a little shy. I wasn't sure what to do, so I held up my Coke bottle and blew on its lip. It made such a pretty sound.

"Sorry about that," Jill apologized upon her return. "I don't know what happened. Now where were we?" She sat down across from me and returned her attention to our lesson. "You're going to wanna place your hand here," she showed me, guiding my hand along the ridges of glass, "and wub—uh hem—sorry."

"Wub?" I laughed. "What is wub?"

"Rub," she corrected me. "Not wub. Rub." Jill seemed to be struggling as she stuck out her tongue and stretched her lips.

"You okay?" I asked.

"Yah. Fine. Now let's keep going."

She continued my Jedi training on the bottle and moved on to a secret covert operation that she claimed was classified by the fat girl government—Deep Throat. For this, she provided two freshly peeled bananas. Oh good, I was hungry!

Jen Ashton

"Thith ith where," she stuttered. "Uh hem—thith ith where." She cleared her throat again. "I mean, *this* is where we learn how to open our throats."

Call me crazy, but it seemed Jill was having a hard enough time just opening her mouth. Her words kept slurring and she was flubbing her sentences. Something wasn't right.

"You sure you're okay?" I asked again.

"Yah, my tongue dust keeps thwelling up. Ith's weird."

"Maybe we should do this another time then?"

"Thur," she lisped. "Ith's kinda hot up here anyway." She wiped the beads of sweat off her brow and we headed back downstairs where I ate my banana.

Jill's condition got progressively worse as the evening came to a close. Her mouth swelled up and she eventually came down with a high fever. I wasn't interested in catching the flu, so I called my dad to pick me up.

*****

Jen Ashton

Jill wasn't at school on Monday. Or Tuesday. Or Wednesday. I was beginning to wonder if my training was over. But finally, on Thursday, Jill showed up to Social Studies—with two fat lips. She sat at the desk behind me.

"Where the hell have you been?" I whispered, turning around to face her. "Oh God! What's wrong with your lips?!!!"

"Cold sores," she answered, matter-of-factly.

"Are they cold?" I inquired, reaching up to touch them.

"Don't!" she scolded me. "They're not cold, dummy. They're just called that. Don't touch them, it's contagious."

"Ew," I cringed. "Is that like *Hermes*?" I had heard about those in health class. There were two types.

"You mean herpes. Hermes was the winged messenger." She retorted.

"That's what I said," I lied. Suddenly, I began to get scared. *Oh God, where did she get them? I hope it wasn't those Coke bottles! I told her to wash those things first.* I couldn't take the suspense any longer. "How'd you get them?"

Jill leaned forward, covering her mouth with her hand, and whispered. It was the quietest I had ever seen her. "Blowjobs."

Well, that was it for me. No French kissing. No anal. And now, there was absolutely no way I was going to blow on boys.

Girls Don't Poop

Jen Ashton

Lesson #9:

EITHER WAY, I LOSE

By the time I had decided I was going to give my body to a boy, I was scared shitless. So far, my choices were eternal damnation or a viral infection. Neither of which sounded too enchanting. Maybe I wasn't cut out for this sort of thing. Or maybe, God had a brilliant plan to make sure I remained a virgin forever. Not that I wanted to be more of a disappointment than I already was to my parents, but if He was counting on me to become a nun, he was sadly mistaken. Jill's Saturday service was more up my alley. With or without the lip fungus.

Once I became comfortable with my odds, I hatched a plan to lose my virginity. His name was also Mike. And—come to think of it—he, too, had unusually large lips. I'm seeing a pattern. Anyway, he was one grade my senior and never gave me the time of day. I was going to have to become a real whore to get his attention, so I enlisted the help of my best friend Alyssa.

Alyssa and I had been inseparable since the sixth grade. Except for when she was grounded; which was always. She lived with her mom; an ex hippy who smoked two packs of Benson and Hedges a day. She was a liberal, but apparently not liberal enough to let Alyssa hang out with me. I was a bad influence. I stole candy bars—something I never really grew out of—and dressed like a boy. Worse still, I took Alyssa to Burger King on Saturday nights.

The Burger King parking lot in our town was the breeding ground for all teenage relationships in the early nineties. Everyone was there—from eight graders to seniors—smoking their Camel Wides and drinking Mountain Dew. You know, just being rebels.

We girls were some of the youngest, so to ensure our coolness we needed a car. We weren't proud, but we ended up soliciting the services of a nerdy junior that Jill was still servicing. He had just gotten his license, and what better way to feel like a man than to have a car full of girls. Ninth grade girls. Lucky for us, Jill always called in the favor, so we always had a ride; complete with a preliminary drive-by so everyone could see us.

Jen Ashton

My guy was guaranteed to be there every weekend. Rain or shine, Mike never missed a night. Burger King was his hangout. If I wanted to lose my virginity, I was going to have to fetch him there. So one Saturday, after taking Alyssa's advice on how to land Mike, she helped me line up a theme song for our drive-by that was sure to set the mood.

"Did you bring the tape?" Jill asked. She got to ride up front. I'm sure she did more than that up front when we weren't in the car.

"Sure did," Alyssa answered, handing Jill the cassette. "Turn it up loud."

Jill slipped the tape into the car stereo and cranked up the volume. "Ready girls? This is my favorite song! Everybody has to sing!"

The nerd could barely see over the steering wheel, but he made sure we swooped in close to the Burger King crowd so they could witness our awesomeness. He was a good chauffer. We were all piled in—Jill, Alyssa, Jessica, me and five other girls—with the windows down. We cranked up the tunes, ready to impress with our sweet serenade of NWA's Automobile song.

"You don't have to front on me, Bitch!" we all sang at the top of our lungs. "Don't be afraid, it's only a dick!" We were so classy.

The song continued as we parked. "If you'll be good to me, oh, I'll be good to you. And we'll both ride home in my automobile!"

The stage was set.

As the car stopped, we all got out; sans Jill. "I'll see you guys in a few," she said, leaning the front seat forward to let us out. "He's gonna take me to get some smokes." We all knew what that meant. She was such a good friend to pay for our ride like that.

Alyssa and I immediately left the others and made our way through the crowd to where Mike lingered. In case he hadn't heard my mating song, I wanted my presence known. We found him standing against a light post, smoking Camels with his best friend Nathan (who happened to be channeling Vanilla Ice that night).

"Hey," I said, walking up in my Timberland slip-ons and scrunchy socks. "What are you boys getting into tonight?" I stared directly at Mike and dropped my shoulder so that my boat-neck shirt slipped down my arm and revealed a little skin. I also dropped my bottom lip and chin, a move I thought made me look sexy.

"You're lookin' at it," Nathan answered, sweeping his hand across the steps shaved in the side of his head. I wasn't even talking to him. I motioned to Alyssa to get rid of him.

"Wanna get a Dr. Pepper?" she asked him. He obliged and they headed into Burger King.

"So..." I stuttered, shuffling my feet on the asphalt. "You got another Camel Wide?"

"Fresh out," Mike shrugged, retrieving his soft pack from his back pocket and crumpling it in front of my face. "Sorry."

"That's cool. I mean, not really, but—like, it's fine that you don't have any left. I wasn't just going to ask for a smoke and leave. So it's still cool. You're cool. We're cool, right?"

"Yeah. We're cool," he smiled. "Take care." And just like that, Mike walked away with my dreams of losing my virginity.

Alyssa returned twenty seconds later with two Dr. Peppers and handed me one. "Where's Mike?" she inquired. Looking around.

"He left. I don't think he's into me." I moped for a minute while I sipped on my straw. "What happened to Nathan?"

"Oh, his girlfriend is here so we made out in the bathroom real fast. I gave him your number and told him to call me later." It was for this exact reason that I had enlisted her help in the first place. She was a pro.

We waited around for awhile looking like losers, but Jill never came back with the car. Without smokes and without boys, there was nothing more to accomplish at Burger King that night, so we hoofed it home. Neither one of us spoke the entire two miles. I was not only heartbroken that I would not be losing my virginity to Mike that night, but I was also dumbfounded at where I went wrong. The song had seemed like such a great idea. I looked at Alyssa. She was deep in thought too. Perhaps she was second-guessing her serenade selection too.

We walked in my house two minutes to curfew. My dad was on the couch watching Cape Fear. "You girls taking the couch tonight?"

"Sure." I plopped my teenage body on the sofa and sighed. "What are you watching?"

Jen Ashton

"It's a new movie with Robert De Niro. It just came out on VHS. It's pretty good."

Alyssa sat down next to me and the three of us watched the rest of the movie together. After the credits, my dad got up and left the living room to us.

"See you girls in the morning." He walked half way up the stairs and paused. "Oh, before I forget. A boy named Nathan called for Alyssa earlier. His number's on the counter."

*****

An hour later my dad was fast asleep and I found myself creeping through my neighbor's yard with Alyssa, wearing all black. Over the hills and through the woods we went. For four straight miles. We climbed fences, ran from dogs and dodged street lights. It was my first official "sneak out."

"So you're sure Mike's gonna be there?" I asked, climbing through a barbed wire fence.

"Yes," she assured me for the hundredth time. "I told Nathan I wasn't coming without you, so he told Mike you wanted to give him your cherry."

"And what did Mike say?" I held the fence open for her to slide through after me.

"He said okay."

We walked for what seemed like another hour, dodging headlights like Indiana Jones as they came up the road, until we reached our destination. Covered in scrapes and bruises from thorn bushes and gravel, we finally arrived at the local electric company; our official meeting spot. It was conveniently surrounded by manicured lawns and gardens; a perfect place for a romantic rendezvous. When we walked up, we found Nathan sitting at a picnic table by himself.

"I thought you said Mike would be here," I whispered.

Alyssa nudged me with her elbow and spoke back through her teeth, "Let me handle it." She took a deep breath and smiled. "Hey, Nathan." She gave him a noogie, sat down and lit up a smoke one of his smokes. "I thought Mike was comin' too."

"He's here." He pointed toward a tree. My eyes strained in the darkness to see Mike standing behind it, taking a leak. I was more relieved than he was.

For the next forty-five minutes, we all sat at the table smoking Nathan's cigarettes. Alyssa and Nathan sat on one side. Her shorts were unzipped and his hand was inside them. Mike and I sat on the other. Our legs were touching. It was an official double date.

"You girls wanna get outta here?" Nathan suggested.

"Where?" I inquired.

"Mike's house. It's just around the corner. We could head over there and hang out in his bedroom. It might be more comfortable."

That was a splendid suggestion, as far as I was concerned. I had never really imagined losing my virginity outdoors, on a lawn, next to a tree where my boy of choice had just pissed. But his bedroom? Now that was more like it! I had often fantasized about rolling around in the sheets with him, making love and cuddling after. We could take the bed. Alyssa and Nathan could take the floor. It would be so romantic; so special.

"Sounds good to me," I announced, standing up and putting out my Camel. "Let's go."

Feeling confident that tonight was the night, I led the pack in the direction that Nathan had pointed, forgetting all about curfew as we walked across the front lawn of the electric company. Suddenly, a pair of headlights turned into the parking lot and shone right on us.

"Hide!" Nathan shouted, diving into the flowerbed.

"Run!" Mike cried out, grabbing my hand and pulling me into a bush. Alyssa tumbled in after me, stepping on my foot.

"Ouch!" I screamed. "Watch where you're stepping."

"Shhh—" Mike shushed us, pulling me closer. His arm wrapped around me. I could feel his chest rising and falling with every breath. It was our first embrace.

The car pulled around and parked. *Shit*, it was a cop; a canine cop. He turned off his lights and got out of the car, leaving the dog inside. Alyssa, Mike and I held our breaths, hoping to keep still enough inside our bush. We didn't want to tip off the cop, or the dog either. Still, we watched in horror through the branches as the officer walked up the sidewalk, closer and closer to where Nathan was laying. My heart was racing. Mike's was too. Within a few steps, the cop would be standing right over him.

"Shit!" Nathan conceded.

The cop turned on his flashlight and scoured the flowerbed. Placing his other hand on his gun, he ordered Nathan to get up. "Who's in there?! You better come outta there with your hands up!"

Nathan rose from the flowers, spitting dirt from his mouth.

"What were you doin' in there? You causin' trouble out here, son?"

"No sir," Nathan answered as the cop frisked him.

"What'r you doing out here so late then?"

"Nothing, sir. Just taking a walk."

"Takin' a walk, huh? In the flowerbed? I'm no fool, son."

"I just wanted some fresh air, sir."

"Yeah right…Nathan," the officer addressed him as he read his ID. "I'll tell you what, son, we've been getting a lot of vandalism in this area. I'm gonna run your name and see if I can't pin it on you."

Just then, Alyssa stepped on a twig. The crack of the branch was enough to startle the dog, which began barking ferociously in the back seat. The cop shone his flashlight in our direction.

"Who's there?!!! You've got three seconds to show yourself before I let my dog out on you!"

Mike pushed me back with his arm. "Stay here," he told me. "I'll go."

"No," I urged. "You'll get busted!" Those were the words that left my lips, but what I was feeling inside was far more tragic. If Mike walked away now, I was going to have to go home, tail between my legs, cherry intact. Again. For the second time in one night. What were the odds?

"He's my best friend," Mike continued. "And besides, it's me…or all of us."

Jen Ashton

I swallowed hard and looked at Alyssa. As much as I didn't want to admit it, it was true. We hadn't been caught yet. I may not lose my virginity tonight, but I wouldn't lose my head either. My dad would kill me if he knew I snuck out. Thank God the cop couldn't see us through the brush. Good thing we dressed like ninjas. I nodded to Mike and the decision was made. And just like that, the boy who was to discover my bush that night, instead walked out of it, with his hands up.

Mike joined Nathan on the curb while the cop ran their names through dispatch. Alyssa and I kept quiet, standing still and breathing once a minute like the stealth ninjas we were. We were waiting for it all to be over so we could begin our return trek home.

But the cop wasn't letting up. He was convinced the boys were vandals or thieves. Anyone who looked like Vanilla Ice had to be a gangster.

Once the officer got out his cuffs, I couldn't watch anymore. I felt bad. The only reason Mike and Nathan were even at the electric company that night was because Alyssa and I had promised them promiscuity. The only thing they were stealing was our integrity. And now they were being arrested. I needed to do something. If I could show Mike that

I cared about him as much as he cared about Nathan, maybe he would actually ask me to be his girlfriend after he took my cherry. I mean, after all, that *would* be ideal.

"I'm going out there," I whispered to Alyssa. "Wish me luck!"

She tried to hold me back, but it was too late. I was already half way to the flowerbed. "Officer! Officer!" I called out, waving my hands in the air. "They're not criminals!" Mike's face turned white with shock, Nathan laughed under his breath and Alyssa stumbled out behind me. "They were just sneaking out to meet *us*."

*****

I knew I was in deep shit when my dad pulled up at two-thirty in the morning to pick us up. He never even knew I was gone. Last he saw me, I was watching TV on the couch, ready for bed. The cop had to call him twice to assure him that it *was* me in custody. When he arrived, my dad talked to the officer for a few minutes, nodding his head in disappointment. I was shamed forever. He wouldn't even look at me. This was not the way I wanted him to meet my soon-to-be-boyfriend.

I sat there on that curb, embarrassed, pondering the thought that I was inevitably going to lose my head before my cherry. Just another cruel joke by God. A tragedy. It wasn't fair. Why was it so dang hard? I lost my homework all the time. I lost my keys, my number 2 pencils, my friends, but for some damned reason—even after two tries in one night—I could *not* lose my virginity. Blasphemy!

Come to find out, the officer knew my dad and had called him to spare us any harsh punishment. Maybe that could be said for the rest of them, but not for me. I knew my dad was going to dish out a grounding that ensured I would be keeping my virginity until I was at least twenty. There was no way Mike was going to wait for me. That was six years! I knew right then and there that our romance was over. And worse, I still had to give him a ride home.

All four of us piled into the back seat and sat in shameful silence. As the officer said goodnight to my father, he told his side of the story.

"You know, Kevin, I didn't even know these kids were up here. I was just coming to pay my electric bill." We all looked at each other in defeat as he chuckled to himself. "But something told me things ain't right as soon as I heard the flowerbed say *shit!*"

Jen Ashton   151

Girls Don't Poop

Jen Ashton

PRELUDE TO ADULTHOOD

Needless to say, growing up hadn't exactly been a picnic for me. Unless, it's normal to pack yourself a basket full of park time condiments like anal lube and tit cream. *Hun, did you bring the hot dogs? Yes, Dear. They're right next to the poodle balls and twelve inch maxi pads, squished between my dignity and virginity.*

Yep, mine was a journey best traveled alone and—for the most part—I did just that. Aside from the smut magazines, an anal-loving housekeeper, some clueless friends and a preaching principal, I pretty much had to separate fact from fiction all on my own. It wasn't easy, but after a few years of desperately searching the card catalog and microfiche at my school library, I found out that China was real, black people do have bones, that you don't pee through your asshole and that Obi Wan Kenobi was not named after a tampon.

In my teenage prime, I finally lost my virginity to a boy whose name was *not* Mike. Turns out then

Jen Ashton   153

name was not a prerequisite to getting into my pants after all. Sex was not what I expected, and it hurt. (I was super-duper quadruple-duper relieved that I had long since ceased my pursuit of anal once I realized this.) But all in all, it wasn't too bad. And I will have to admit, it was more romantic than my previously planned rite of passage with Mike. My new beau and I did it to Too Short.

With sex out of the way, you'd think I naturally progressed to marijuana, then crack, and then eventually to selling babies on the black market. But that never happened—except for part of it. High or not though, I never did take up blowjobs. I had been scared straight and decided to throw those right into the *sinful pleasures of monkeys and gays* category. In fact, it wouldn't actually be until my late twenties that I would revisit my oral dilemma. If you want to know how that worked out, there are a few stories about me and a man I called Popsicle in my previous book, "Turds in the Punch Bowl". But, finish this book first.

If you're still here, you'd be happy to know that—aside from a shit-ton of terrible advice, a few ridiculous attempts to be more grown up than I was and a short stint working at a pizza dive for a man who wanted me to call him Daddy—I survived my teens. I graduated from high school early and moved across the country to a lovely little state called California. I was an adult now. I lived on my own and I had a job. One that had nothing to do with blowing, newspapers or pizza parlors. You could say, I had found heaven…or had I? Turns out, there were plenty of gays in Long Beach.

I fit right in. With my Dickie pants and wallet chain, wifebeater tanks and nose rings, I was a regular hipster hanging with the other sinners. If you blinked, you might've mistaken me as one of the effeminate boys. I was *that* cool. But one day, somewhere between my testosterone-filled obsessions with White Zombie and Rage Against the Machine, I heard the music of a brand new feminist group called the Spice Girls. It changed my life. While Japan was busy producing a new thing called a DVD and Bill Clinton was lining up his staff of oral—uh hem, sorry, frog in my throat—*oval* office staff, I decided I might need to get more serious about this whole femininity thing. I'll tell you what I want, what I really, really want. I wanted some girlfriends. Real ones.

So that's what I did. I ditched the homos and found myself some girls. Not the Butch Cassidy type like Jessica. Real, beautiful, feminine, dainty girls. At least that's what they looked like on the outside. The women of my adult life would prove

Jen Ashton   155

to yield even more life lessons that I would take with me on the home stretch to womanhood.

Lesson #10:

DON'T THINK OUTSIDE THE BOX

I met Amanda at a coffee shop when she almost stepped on me.

Amanda was a beautiful Amazonian brunette whose long legs went all the way up and made an ass out of themselves. She also smelled like cat piss, but no one seemed to mind. She was hot, funny and, well, really leggy. Not only did her gams go far with the boys, but they went far up her skirts too. Come to think of it, I wasn't even sure she had a butt. Her legs may have actually just extended right into her back.

At 5'4" I only came up to her knees. As she stumbled over me, I found myself face to face with her beautifully sculpted calves. Stunned, I slowly panned up her body. Five minutes later, our eyes met.

"I am *so* sorry," she apologized, bending down to pat me on the head. "I didn't see you down there."

Jen Ashton

"It's okay."

"Don't be silly," she assured me. "Let me buy you a coffee."

From that moment on, Amanda and I were best friends. An unlikely pair, we began meeting at the coffee shop every day; she in her feminine dresses and perfectly groomed locks, me in my cargo pants and thrift store t-shirts. People probably thought we were a couple, and it was pretty apparent that I wore the pants in our relationship. We would sit outside on the patio chairs all night, chatting and laughing, sipping on our thirty cent coffees and ten cent refills. It was a cheap good time.

The one thing that Amanda and I *did* have in common was that we were both broke. Perpetually. I was living with a guy at the time. I had no job, no car and no money. All I had was a bed to sleep in and a boyfriend who frequently left for weeks on commercial fishing trips. I scraped by each day on change I found around the house or borrowed from my neighbors. Usually, by the end of the day, I was fresh out of what little I had. I often considered myself lucky when I had enough to buy a $0.39 taco for dinner. Amanda, on the other hand, at least had a car and her own apartment. She didn't work either and to my knowledge, her parents helped pay her bills. We were young, unemployed and free. It was awesome.

Every morning around 10 a.m. Amanda pulled up in her 1995 convertible Chrysler LeBaron and honked.

"Wake up, Short Round!" she yelled.

I rolled out of bed, got dressed in a hurry and—pushing aside month-old trash and dirty laundry—jumped in her flashy sports car.

"I've got three dollars," she informed me. "Hungry?"

"You bet!"

We rolled into the parking lot of 7-Eleven in style; top down, hair flowing in the wind, music blaring and trash flying out the back. We were two girls on the prowl. For food. Three dollars happily provided two Big Gulps for $0.99 each and a 2-for-1 hotdog deal. We always made sure to load up on nacho cheese, jalapenos and any other free condiment. Just in case we got hungry later. She was such a good friend to feed me like that, and in turn I would pick up our coffee tab. It was the healthiest symbiotic relationship I've ever had. Except for the smell.

Jen Ashton   159

Not only was Amanda's car filled with trash and clothes, but her apartment was a mess too. It would be months, though, before I found this out. I had always assumed this to be true—where there's smoke, there's fire—but never knew for sure until I was finally invited over. And even that was a fluke.

"Shit," she cursed as her hot coffee spilled onto her lap. "That's gonna stain."

We left the coffee shop and headed over to her apartment; in style.

The first time I walked in, I wasn't sure if I was supposed to step up onto the piles of clothes to make my way to the kitchen, or if I should try to blaze a path through them—at least Indy's sidekick had a machete, I only had my bare hands. I chose the latter, but half way through, I hit a wall—of stench. The most putrid smell of cat urine and rotten food smacked me in the face so hard I thought I had been hit by a garbage truck. What the hell *was* that?

I pinched my nose and a brief tour of her place revealed crusty dishes, rotten fruit and milk, dirty clothes, musty furniture and five kittens. (Creative felines, I might add. They definitely thought *outside* the box.) The floor was covered in cat shit and urine stains. I can't say the couch and bed looked much different. I couldn't imagine where

Jen Ashton

Amanda sat down in there, let alone slept. I watched as she scoured through piles of soiled clothes in her bedroom, pulling a sleeve until it revealed an entire garment, wrinkled and stained. She did this a few times, tossing the clothes aside if they weren't a suitable match to what she already had on that day.

The kittens cried and clawed at her feet until she found a replacement dress.

"Oh!" she squealed, sending the kittens scattering in all directions. "This is perfect!"

She held the dress up into the sunlight that strained to pour through her mini blinds. It was a beautiful pale blue, cotton dress...covered in cat piss. Amanda leaned in and smelled it.

"Oh?!" she flinched, catching a whiff of the potent stench. She paused for a moment and smiled. "Nothing a little perfume can't cure!"

What?!!! Was she serious? That dress was filthy! It was covered in cat piss and yellow stains that expanded out into dark brown rings of petrified urine crystals. It wasn't wearable. Not just now, but ever.

"You're seriously considering wearing that?" I asked, horrified.

"Yeah," she frowned. "It's fine. I'll just scrub the stains with a little dish soap and spray some perfume on it. It'll be good as new." She disappeared into the bathroom with her pale blue litter box in hand.

Moments later she returned wearing the litter box. I couldn't believe my eyes. She looked gorgeous. Her long legs led my gaze up to the hem of her dress. And there it was. Aside from a few wet spots that were quickly drying from the California heat, the dress looked brand new. By golly, she was right.

"See," she bragged, turning to show off her figure. "Just like new!"

"I would've never guessed."

"Well, you should've just trusted me," she pledged. "I do it all the time. Nobody knows the difference."

For a second, I considered the fact that Amanda may have just been a poverty-stricken young woman who was forced to cut corners because she didn't have enough money to do her laundry at the local Laundromat. Or perhaps, footing the bill for her best friend's lunches at 7-Eleven had led her to having to make sacrifices in other parts of her life;

Jen Ashton

like doing her laundry. Maybe the kitten ate her quarters. These all seemed like rational explanations. Surely, she wasn't just that disgusting. And please, don't call me Shirley.

Shining like a brand new quarter freshly shit out by an unsuspecting kitten, Amanda suggested we head back to the coffee shop. I thought that was a great idea. If our coffee cups were still hidden behind the cabinet in the girl's bathroom, we could use them to get ten cent refills. I didn't notice on the way over—mostly because the top was down— but, even though the dress looked great now, the ammonia-like aroma of cat piss was beginning to overpower the essence of her CK One. She probably should've used my Drakkar.

"Hey, boys," Amanda flirted, stepping out of her car like a 1980's GUESS ad vixen. Her limbs extended out like branches of a tall, sexy oak tree. Everyone took notice. She moved in slow motion—or maybe that's just the way I remember it—slowly stepping onto the pavement with her six-inch heels. Her brunette waves were bouncing in the wind and her sunglasses reflected the rays of the California sun back onto her spectators. Her lips were red and puckered, screaming *Kiss me, you fools!* She really was a sight to behold.

And then there was me. I trailed behind her Goddess-ness, wearing tan utility slacks, Chuck

Taylors and an old tee that was printed for a high school swim team I had never even heard of. It was on sale for $1.29 and it served as a perfect marketing strategy for one night stands. It simply read *Dive In*. At the very least, it was a conversation piece, so I wore it once a week.

After retrieving our mugs, we walked up to the counter and stood in line for our refills. The fragrant aroma of coffee and pastries filled the air; combined with the slow grind of the beans, the steaming milk, the churning dishwasher behind the counter and the melodic tunes of Mazzy Star playing over the speakers. There was something so alluring about coffee houses. One day I would save up enough money to try one of those fancy things called a latte.

"Ew," one patron winced. "What's that smell?" She fanned the air in her immediate vicinity. I figured someone farted. A man, of course. Woman don't fart.

"Something stinks," a barista observed. "Did you just sanitize the sinks?"

"I haven't gotten to them yet," another barista answered. "Why?"

"I just got a whiff of something strong. Like ammonia."

Jen Ashton

"Smells like fertilizer," a man behind us chimed in. "I smell it too."

Suddenly, everyone in line was talking about the potent stench that was wafting through the café like a cloud of green smoke; the ones you see in the cartoons. Sans the floating image of skull and crossbones, it did reek of poisonous gas. No one seemed to be able to pinpoint its origin, though Amanda and I seemed to be standing in the middle of said frenzy. Amanda kept smiling, looking as effervescent as ever. I, on the other hand, knew exactly what stunk around there.

It didn't take long for the others to catch on.

"It's coming from this area," one coffee-sipping hippy announced. He pointed awfully close to wear Amanda was standing.

"That's what I thought, too," another patron agreed. "But it comes and goes in waves. It will be really strong one second and completely disappear the next."

I glanced at Amanda to take note. Sure enough, whenever she shifted her hips to stabilize her stance on those tall stilts of hers, her dress released a wave of toxicity. I suddenly felt bad for complaining about my deviated septum for the last five years. The fact that half of my nose was

Jen Ashton   165

functionless meant I was only subjected to half the smell. Lucky me.

"There it is again," the barista remarked. "Something's not right. I wonder if we have a gas leak."

"Should I call the gas company?" the cashier offered.

"It's Saturday. They won't be open," said the barista, shooting down the idea. "We'll have to call the police."

As the cashier finalized her current sale, the gentlemen behind us tapped Amanda on the shoulder.

"Ma'am?" he addressed her politely. "Excuse me, Ma'am, but you have something on the back of your dress."

"I do?" she exclaimed, trying to turn around and view her own derriere. "What is it?"

"Just a stain," he observed. "I wasn't sure if you knew it was there or not. It looks like coffee. You might have sat in some."

"Oh my God," Amanda mumbled through her teeth, staring me down like it was my fault. "Jen, why didn't you tell me? Is it bad?"

I took a step back and glanced over at Amanda's ass. I tried not to show the surprise on my face as I looked back up at her. "You should probably go to the bathroom." I told her. "It's bad."

After examining herself in the mirror, Amanda asked for my assistance in her getting the hell out of there. Fast. We devised a plan to sneak her past the many suitors awaiting her return outside. That's if they didn't see the stain on her glamorous walk in. *Oh God! Had they all noticed?*

"Go get my car," she strategized. "Pull it around back and I'll meet you in the alley."

"I can't," I replied. I shrugged, knowing I was about to disappoint her. "I don't have my license."

"Who the hell cares? You're just reversing into the alley. Now, go!"

"I can't."

"What? Why?"

"I don't know how to drive." I finally admitted.

"But you're nineteen."

"I know, but I never took driver's ed. I've never driven a car before."

"Fuck!" she shouted, stomping her foot in defeat. "You're just gonna have to cover me then." She opened the bathroom door and instructed me to stay close as she looked both ways before darting.

As the police sirens echoed in the city backdrop and the baristas politely ushered the patrons outside due to the potential gas leak, Amanda tried looking casual as she walked to her flashy automobile parked right smack dab in front of the coffee shop with her boyish-looking best friend attached to her ass. I might as well have been hugging her leg like a toddler as we made that short trek to the car. I was suspiciously close to her. Not to mention, dangerously close to the hazardous stain that was probably emitting some form of radiation.

I walked her to the car, where she slid into the driver's seat and sighed with relief.

"Hurry!" she yelled. "Get in!"

I ran around the back of the car as she fired up the engine and we peeled out of there. Just as the police arrived.

*****

Two months later, Amanda was evicted from her apartment. It was declared condemned. I agreed to help her move if she would teach me how to drive. Boy, did I get the short end of that stick. I showed up on moving day with a radiation suit and a shovel. The kittens were sent to a shelter and what clothes were salvageable were spared. The rest…well, I'd really like to block it out. I saw things that day that I would never even expect to see at the city dump. Most shit makes its way to the sewer. In Amanda's world though, the only person pooping in the proper place was Amanda. And I'm hesitant to even make that statement.

I learned a lot that day; about cleanliness and personal hygiene, turn signals and parallel parking, where feces can actually end up if you don't keep an eye on it and how appearances can be deceiving. But most importantly, I seriously began to rethink a motto I had believed in my entire creative life. *Think outside the box* no longer had anything to do with *thinking* as far as I was concerned. From now on, I wasn't going to be too worried if all my good ideas happened to get flushed down the toilet.

Girls Don't Poop

Jen Ashton

Lesson #11:

FAKE IT TIL YOU MAKE IT

Speaking of good ideas, cue Kelly.

"Pack your bags. We're going to Las Vegas!" she shouted over the phone.

"When?"

"Tonight. We're flying out at seven."

"A girl's weekend?" I inquired.

"Nope. We're going with Ron."

Kelly was a vivacious little blonde that I met in Los Angeles. She was fun, quirky and dumb as shit. I was under the impression that she only had two brain cells. The problem was that one was lost and the other was looking for it. As absent-minded as they came, she was still a good friend. I joined her at the hip and we hit the LA party scene at the ripe old age of twenty one.

We had met Ron—a hotshot record exec—earlier that year at a release party at Capitol Records. He had signed a few new hip-hop artists and made a pretty good name for himself. He was tall, dark (as in skin, not Galactic Empire) and not-so-handsome. He was also old. Not crusty old, but forty-ish; which is a fogey to a twenty-something. Nevertheless, Ron was taken by the dynamic duo that was Jen and Kelly, so he continued to invite us to party after party.

"Business or pleasure?" I asked.

"Ron's business. Our pleasure," she assured me.

We weren't exactly sure if Ron sold records or drugs. But it didn't matter. He never involved us in his dealings. We were just there for the party. An overnight trip to Vegas meant he had a meeting and we were off to the hot tub. After that, we would accompany him to a VIP table at the best club in town and dance our asses off. He never expected anything else out of us. Maybe he was dumb too.

"Cool, see you at the airport at six." I hung up the phone and packed my bag.

Jen Ashton

I met Kelly at the Southwest check-in. She was so cute, standing there on the curb in her sundress and sandals. She was an inch shorter than me—which may, or may not, have qualified her as a legal midget—with big blue eyes and long blonde hair. She was what big-boned women call *petite*. Even in the torso. I'll admit, I hadn't been blessed in the breast quadrant either, but Kelly seemed to have been overlooked completely. Never the one to complain, with her perfect smile and airy personality, Kelly made do with what she did have—money. Not very much, but enough to purchase a new product on the market called an insert (a solid silicone slab of fake tit, complete with an erect nipple).

She flagged me down and waved her arms in the air wildly. It didn't take long for the inserts to wiggle to edges of her top and peek out the sides of her sundress.

"Oops!" she squealed, tucking them back in. "These things never stay in." She walked up and hugged me, pressing them firmly against my chest. "Good to see you."

"You too," I greeted her. "Maybe next time you should try wearing a bra. They might stay in better."

"No way!" she shrieked. "Then you wouldn't be able to see the nipples. Look," she insisted, pulling her sundress tight to her new slabs. "It looks like I'm cold!" She laughed excitedly. She was truly thrilled about her revelation.

"Except it's ninety degrees out," I reminded her.

"Doesn't matter," she scoffed. "They're not for you. *You* don't have to like them."

Just then Ron walked up. "Don't have to like what?"

"Kelly's tits." I caught him up on the conversation.

Ron looked down at Kelly's tiny physique and her supple breasts. "Well, I like 'em!" Shocking.

*****

The three of us checked in at the curb and made our way to the terminal. In the days before heightened security and racial profiling, we slipped through the scanners effortlessly with a black man and an unassuming blonde armed with silicone bombs. To our delight, we were seated within minutes in row 17; seats D, E and F. Ron took the window seat and I took the aisle (so I was closer to the exit 'in case of emergency'—not the dad-dying kind, but the everyone-might-be-dying sort.) Kelly ended up squished between us.

"I hope they serve dinner on this plane," she said with dim optimism. "I'm starving."

"I doubt it," I argued. "It's only a forty-minute flight."

"Well, they have to at least serve us peanuts. Right?"

I was quickly reminded that a small bag of ten honey roasted peanuts might actually be an adequate meal for her. "I'm sure they'll have peanuts. Don't worry."

Kelly calmed down, hopeful her belly would be full by the time we landed, and Ron turned his attention to his carry-on—Dub Magazine. He traveled light. We were officially all settled in for the long flight over the Sierra Nevada Mountains. We taxied, we took off, and ten minutes later we were descending into Las Vegas.

"Ladies and gentlemen," the captain announced over the intercom, "we'd like to thank you for flying Southwest Airlines today. We are now on our final descent into Las Vegas. Please return your seatbacks and tray tables to their upright positions. We will arrive at our destination at approximately 7:45pm Pacific Time."

"What?!!!" Kelly screamed. "We're there already? What about my peanuts?"

"Maybe they didn't have time." I tried to get her to relax, but her stomach was talking.

"That's bullshit," she argued. "They *have* to feed us. They never even came by for drinks! What kind of operation is this?"

"A short one," Ron commented, lifting his eyes from an informative article on page 23: Chicks Dig Chrome.

"Not fair." Kelly whined. "I wanted some peanuts."

A few seconds later Kelly lowered her tray table and pulled a plastic fork and knife from her purse. She removed one of her inserts and slapped it down in front of us. Ron lowered his research.

"What the hell is that?" he asked in fear.

"Kelly's tit," I informed him.

"Looks like a chicken cutlet," he observed.

"I thought it looked like a filet of flounder," I added.

"Shut up guys," Kelly interjected, slapping Ron across the face with her silicone paddle. "You're hurting my feelings." Apparently her falsies were just as sensitive as the real thing. We both looked at her in confusion as she reached up and pressed the call button.

"What are you doing?" Ron asked, rubbing his cheek.

"Getting my peanuts," she assured us, smiling confidently.

A few seconds later, the flight attendant arrived. "Uh hi, Miss," Kelly began, cringing her cute little face. "Um, I don't think I ordered this."

The stewardess looked down at Kelly's flounder-tit in horror. "What is that?" she inquired, leaning toward down to get a better look at the tiny mosquito bump protruding from the center of the mysterious chicken cutlet that she never served the passenger in seat 17E.

"I'm not sure," Kelly played, lifting her knife and fork. She struggled to slice the filet. "But I can't even cut into it. Do you think maybe I could get some peanuts instead?"

"Sure," the flight attendant reluctantly agreed, returning moments later with two bags of peanuts. Whoever said you can't use your assets to get what you want?

*****

After checking into our suite at the Hard Rock Hotel, Ron showered and left for his meeting. Flounder-Tits and I instinctively raided the min-bar and got ready for the hot tub.

"Should I leave these in?" she inquired, walking out of the bathroom in her French-cut suit with her filets stuffed inside her bikini top.

"Only if you plan on cooking dinner while we're out there."
"Do you really think the hot tub will boil them?" She was cuter than she was smart. Kinda like Kimmy.

"No. I don't. Grab the camera. Let's go."

We found the hot tub empty of other hotel guests and slipped right into the bubbles. It didn't take more than thirty seconds for Kelly's cutlets to float out of her bikini top and disappear into the foam.

"Oh shit!" she yelled. "My tits are gone!"

We scrambled around the water, scanning the spa with our eyes and hands, looking for Kelly's lost assets.

"Found one!" I shouted, holding it up.

"Found the other!" she echoed back. "Maybe we should leave these over here so I don't lose 'em again." She retrieved my filet and set them on the ground. The silicone sisters were reunited again. This time, *outside* the hot tub.

We spent the next two hours lounging in the boiling tub of people soup and posing for sexy pictures. Nobody was around, so when that got old, we took off our tops and shot some that were more risqué. When *that* got boring, we threw Kelly's tits back in the pool and tried for some artistic shots of a project we called "Floating Filets." We were having our own version of fun. Until, a security guard showed up and pissed on our parade.

"Ladies, you know the hot tub is closed?"

"Oh, sorry," Kelly apologized, grabbing her bikini top to cover her bee stings.

"I'll need you to get out," he continued, folding his arms. "Pool opens back up at six a.m."

"Aw, c'mon," I begged. "We're not hurting anyone."

But he stood his ground. "I'll wait while you get your things."

"Fine," I agreed. We were in big trouble; the kind that warrants a roid head to give you the stink eye and enforce what little authority he has. He was probably bullied in school. Suits him right for wanting to be a hall monitor. I knew his type. I grabbed my top off the rail and tied it back on as Mr. My-Mom-Didn't-Hug-Me stood over us and watched. He helped us gather our towels and escorted out of the pool area. Good boy. He got a red star for completing his assignment.

*****

Later that night, Kelly and I were getting ready for the club while waiting for Ron to return.

"Oh my God!!!" Kelly screamed in horror. She came running into my bathroom covering her chest.

"What?!!!"

"My tits!!!"

"What about them?"

"They're gone! My tits are gone! I can't find them anywhere." She was frantic and sweating. "Shit, Jen! Where are my tits?"

"They're here. We'll find them," I said calmly, wishing I had Angela Lansbury's number. She would surely be better at solving the case of the missing filet than any Las Vegas detective. Flounder, she wrote.

Kelly went crazy, tearing apart the room, while I called Ron. "Hey, are you on your way?"

"Yah, why?"

"Can you stop by Lost and Found on your way up?"

"Sure. What'd ya lose?"

"Kelly's tits. I think we left them in the pool."

Twenty minutes later, there was a knock on the door. "Did someone call a doctor?" a man's voice called from the other side.

Kelly and I both walked out of our rooms and stared at each other in confusion. We ran down the hall and listened through the threshold.

"*Who* is it?" Kelly questioned.

"Doctor Frankenstein," Ron mumbled in a low growl. "I heard someone lost their tits."

Kelly shot me a look. Unlike her other pleasantly empty stares of stupidity, this one spoke of joy. I nodded and smiled. "I had Ron pick up your filets. You left them in the hot tub."

Kelly couldn't open the door fast enough. It swung open and she screamed. Ron was standing there in a smock—that he must've also picked up from Lost and Found—covered in ketchup, holding a knife and a glass of ice with a ketchup-covered filet inside. One eye was covered with a makeshift eye patch made of the other silicone insert and a bandana.

"Hurry, nurse!" he shouted at me. "We need to get his patient subdued so we can sew her tit back on! Lay her down on the bed and prepare her for surgery!"

Laughing, I pulled Kelly to the bed where Ron met us, holding the cutlet on ice. "Where'd you find it?" I asked curiously.

"I stole it from a stripper," he joked, looking down at his bloody smock. "It wasn't easy. As you can see, she put up a good fight."

"But doctor, you only have one tit," I played along. "What about the other?"

"She'll have to make do with one. We can put it in the middle." He cackled like an old witch, holding up his knife. "We must hurry, though. This thing's been on ice for an hour now. They don't stay fresh for long. Nurse! Subdue the patient!"

Kelly was a good sport while Ron and I pretended to perform surgery on her. In the end, she was pretty happy to have her cutlets back before the club. I just wish she would've been smart enough to wash the ketchup off first.

*****

Jen Ashton   183

Years later, I ran into Flounder-Tits at Snoop Dogg's video shoot for his 1999 smash hit Bitch Please. She had foregone the filets altogether and opted for a boob job. *What?!! Bitch, please!* She looked fantastic. Top-heavy, but fantastic. Kelly had finally invested in some tits that—no matter how clueless she was—and bra or not—turbo hot tub jets and all—she couldn't lose. It was at that moment, as I ogled over her perfectly round voluptuous breasts, that I regretted spending my savings on that tit cream years ago. If I had just kept reselling stolen candy bars all these years, I'd probably have enough money to purchase a pair of perfect implants too.

"Floating Filets"

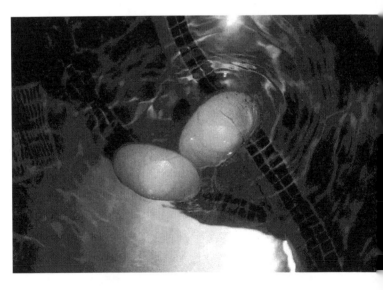

Jen Ashton

Lesson #12:

REVENGE IS SWEET

The Snoop Dogg video led me to the next episode—Dr. Dre's Next Episode—which, in turn, led me to the next chapter of my life.

While George Lucas was filming Star Wars Episode II: Attack of the Clones, I too was writing my own story of transition to the Dark Side. Armed with a new pair of tits (compliments of Dr. Augmentation), I could be found shaking my stuff in every hip-hop club in town. I was draped in bling, rollin' on dubs and still no closer to looking like a lady. Rather than becoming the whitest Nubian queen this side of the Sahara, I dressed like a thug. Baggy jeans, long tee shirts, baseball caps—this was my gear. But despite my gangsta attire, my vanilla milkshake still brought all the boys to the yard.

Contrary to Anakin Skywalker's slow discovery of the seduction that is the Dark Side, I just dived right in, and it quickly became my

Jen Ashton   185

kryptonite. Chocolate is addictive, according to a 2010 Neuroscience case study of white mice. I was no different, no more resistant. I was white and I craved the chocolate too. I was a bona fide chocoholic, sampling boys from mocha to dark. They loved me and I loved them; which is weird considering I had inflated my breasts, but had neglected my ass. I was a top-heavy, flat-butt wigger chick that dressed like a dude. Classy.

That all changed one night at a club when a friend of mine introduced me to a guy named Mike. I know what you're thinking, but no, this was not any kind of reunion with the French-kissing boy who never took me back, or the Mike who agreed to take my virginity so his friend could get laid. This was a brand new Mike. One who was tall, handsome and had those deliciously large lips that I love so much. His only downfall? He was white. Well, half-white, but that was *really* white considering the dark places I had been lately.

"I'm Mike. What's your name?" he asked, holding out his hand to introduce himself.

I high-fived him. "Yo, yo, yo. My name's Jennie J." I tipped my hat and pulled off my yellow sunglasses to get a better look at him. Clubs were so bright back then.

Jen Ashton

Mike just laughed at me. I couldn't tell if he was amused or amazed by my ridiculousness. Still, he pried into my life. "So," he yelled above the dancehall reggae blasting through the speakers, "What's your story?"

"My story? Yo, is that how you address a lady?"

Mike shot me a deadpan stare. His gaze dropped, panning down to my Chronic 2001 t-shirt and baggy sweatpants. He finally stopped when he reached my Adidas sports sandals. "You're a funny girl," he retorted and walked away.

What?!! Did I just get rejected? By a white guy? No way. Wasn't happening. I stopped dancing and walked over to the bar where Mike was standing in line for a drink. "Yo? Why'd you leave?"

"You're not my type," he told me, matter-of-factly.

"I'm not *your* type? You've got to be kidding me! You're the one who's white!'

"What's that supposed to mean?" he asked, looking at my porcelain skin.

"The blacker the berry, the sweeter the juice? Ever heard that saying?"

"Yes, but in case you didn't notice, *Jennie J.,* you're white too."

No one had ever put it to me that way. I was instantly smitten. Mike and his big lips became my new obsession. Mike, Mike, Mike. I'm hungry, I'll call Mike. I'm lonely, I'll call Mike. I want to look cool talking on my brand new Nokia cell phone while walking down Hollywood Boulevard, I'll call Mike. He quickly got over my gangsta slang and I inevitably accepted his Caucasian heritage. Despite our differences, we had two things in common. We both loved hip-hip and we both loved sex. We spent every night together, dancing our asses off and screwing each other's brains out. We had a perfect relationship.

As with any "opposites attract" partnership, the perfection didn't last long. One Sunday afternoon while shopping on Melrose with my girlfriend Jules, I had what ended up being the first of a series of horrible, terrible, no good, very bad ideas.

Horrible, Terrible, No Good, Very Bad Idea # 1:

"We should swing by Mike's house on the way home," I mentioned.

"Does he live close by?" Jules asked. She was driving.

"Yep, right around the corner. We could pop in and say hi, stay for a few." What I meant was 'I could screw him real quick while you sit in the living room watching football on his big screen.'

Jules and I hopped in her 1989 Toyota FX hatchback and sat in the oh-so-calming LA traffic. An hour and five blocks later we pulled onto Mike's street. We had the radio up and the windows down, singing R. Kelly's Fiesta. It was a perfect day. Until we pulled up to Mike's house and found an unidentified car in the driveway.

"Whose car is that?" I asked Jules. As if she knew. She had never even met Mike.

"It's not Mike's?"

"No. His is in front of us." I pointed to the Escalade parallel-parked along the curb.

"Maybe he has a friend over to watch the game. Let's go in."

We parked along the street behind Mike's SUV and started to walk up the drive. Mike's windows were open and the game was on. I was beginning to think maybe Jules was right. My suspicions of

Jen Ashton   189

the car in the driveway belonging to another woman were beginning to fade. But, just as my confidence returned, I heard the undeniably familiar sound indicating that Mike was most definitely in his house, on his couch, with another woman—dying.

"Oh! Oh! Oh! Oh God, Mike!"

Jules looked at me as I stood there in shock, my heart racing and blood boiling. I covered my mouth to keep from puking. Jules grabbed my arm and whisked me back to the car, leaving my heart to shatter into pieces on Mike's driveway.

"Oh my God. Oh my God. Oh my God," I repeated. It wasn't Mike that was going to die. It was me.

"Shit, Jen," Jules panicked, shifting into gear and getting us the hell out of there. "What do you want me do?"

"Just drive," I told her.

After an hour of winding through West Hollywood streets, Jules finally pulled over. "You should confront him," she suggested.

I shot her a look that said she was crazy. But wait a minute. *Should* I confront him? Maybe...I should. And that led to –

Horrible, Terrible, No Good, Very Bad Idea # 2:

"What would I even say? He's not technically my boyfriend, Jules."

"You don't say anything. You just show up. Let him figure out what to say."

"I don't know. This whole thing is making me sick to my stomach. Can we go to a gas station? I need to go to the bathroom."

Jules drove us a few blocks to a Marathon station. I grabbed a key from the clerk and hurriedly walked around back to the restroom. My stomach was bubbling from the stress and my butt was sweating. By the time I sat down on the toilet, I wasn't sure if I needed to poop or puke. I was so heartbroken. With my pants around my ankles and my head in my hands—I didn't defecate, and I didn't throw up—I cried instead.

In this moment I realized how much I had cared for Mike. I may have even loved him. *How could he do this? I thought we had a good thing going.* The echoes of Ms. Stupid Car crept into my thoughts again. *Oh! Oh! Oh!* I felt sick again. My stomach gurgled. Mike clearly didn't feel the same for me if he was screwing some low-class pigeon in the middle of the afternoon—on a Sunday, even! The nerve! That double sinner. And what about me? What about *us*? Mike's afternoon delight made it painfully clear that he really didn't give a shit.

He might not give a shit, but, as it turns out, I did.

Horrible, Terrible, No Good, Very Bad Idea # 3:

A wash of revenge suddenly enveloped my body in that Marathon bathroom that Sunday afternoon. After eyeing a discarded Burger King cup in the trash can , I hatched an idea. The kind of idea that can only come from the bowels of a woman scorned. It was a whopper. Literally. I took that cup, peeled off the lid, and let my emotions flow. Every last inch of dirty, filthy, smelly emotion, until that cup was full. The Force was definitely strong in me.

I ran out of the bathroom holding my arm out, waving my steaming cup of poo. "Go, Jules! Go!" I shouted as I jumped in the passenger seat and held my cup out the window.

"Where?!! Where are we going?" she questioned frantically, punching the clutch.

Jen Ashton

"Back to Mike's!"

The ride was somewhat silent until Jules mustered up the courage to investigate. "You gonna tell me what's in the cup, Jen? Please don't tell me it's what I think it is."

"I'll give you two guesses." I smiled. "First hint, it's warm."

"Ew!!!" she screamed. "That's fucked up!" She laughed so hard I think she farted.

Jules slammed the gas and tried to get us across town as fast she could. There we were, two hot girls driving through Beverly Hills on a beautiful Sunday afternoon, heading over to my lover's house with a hot cup of steaming poo hanging out the window.

"What are you going to do with it?" Jules asked hesitantly, making a wide turn to keep from spilling the contents of my cup.

"I don't know," I admitted. "I haven't thought that far ahead yet."

"Well, you better figure it out fast. We're coming up on his street."

We pulled along the street and parked behind Mike's Escalade. I was flushed with nerves. I thought I might need to poo some more.

"Shit! What do I do, Jules?" I was having second thoughts.

"Dump it on that pigeon's car!" she suggested. I had never heard her use slang before. Good girl.

"*Her* car? No way. How about *his*?"

<u>Horrible, Terrible, No Good, Very Bad Idea # 4:</u>

Before I go on, I just have to say: don't judge me. You've been here before, and you know it. But most of you have that thing that says "oh, maybe that's a horrible, terrible, no good, very bad idea." I usually have that. But that day—and I'm not proud of it—I'd left it in my other pair of Filas.

I stepped out of the car—careful not to lose any of the shit I gave about my relationship with Mike—and walked over to his beautiful white Cadillac Escalade. His pride and joy. His status in the world of all things hip hop. The familiar moans of my lover still played in the background as they were joined by the high-pitched squeals of another woman enjoying my Caucasian lover. Hearing them only made things worse. I was flushed with anger. I was fuming—and so was my Burger King cup.

I walked up to Mike's truck, climbed on the roof in broad daylight and dumped my large chocolate Burger King smoothie onto the windshield. It ran down the glass and dispersed across the hood. I placed my hands on my hips and stood there in all my glory. *I declare, by the Castle Jen Skull, I have the power!!!*

Empowered by my shower of poo, I climbed down and rejoined Jules in the car.

"You need to put this on the windshield too," she whispered secretly. She handed me a piece of paper. While I had been dumping my emotions all over Mike's car, Jules had scribbled a note with a sharpie from her glove box. It read:

Beware of the Pigeons!

I grabbed it out of her hand and ran over to Mike's shitty ride. I lifted up the windshield wiper and snapped it back with the note underneath. Serves him right for parking under power lines.

Jules and I drove half way down the lane and parked. We opened her hatchback and took our front row seats to the show. Any minute now, Mike would come walking out and see the shit on his truck. Any minute now...

They say revenge is a dish best served cold, but I had really hoped mine would be delivered steaming hot. But have no fear, Jules and I waited three hours, snacking on old beef jerky and Twizzlers with our feet dangling over the pavement, before Mike and his chicken-head quit screwing and finally came up for air. By that time, rest assured, my revenge was definitely cold. Jules and I laughed our asses off in the tiny trunk of her old beater that day. Mike discovered the shit on his windshield was too big and too dark to have originated from the birds above, leaving him to wallow in a pile of his own vomit. Ms. Stupid Car, on the other hand, seemed to have quite the giggle herself, just before she slapped him. What...a love story.

Jen Ashton

Lesson #13:

KNOW YOUR LIMIT

There comes a time in every young tomboy's life when she needs to stop giving a shit and just accept that she is, in fact, a girl. For me, it was when I was flagged by the U.S. Postal Service for mailing human feces to another cheating boyfriend. (What can I say, it was a long distance relationship.) Lucky for me, it wasn't a federal offense, and I was simply just asked to put a bio hazard sticker on it next time.

Lucky for my future boyfriends, there would be no next time. I was in my mid twenties now and it was time to grow up. I finally realized that no matter how many birthday wishes I wasted, no matter how many shooting stars I saw, I was never going to grow a penis and become my sister's brother. Not without surgery, anyway. The time had come. I needed to hang up the Kangol hat, put on a dress and embrace my femininity once and for all.

My journey to womanhood started—and ended—with the very same person. Mega Margarita Mary.

Mary and I became friends the typical way two girls get together. "Hey! Are you sleeping with my boyfriend?" I wasn't, and so best friends we became. She took me under her wing, helped me shop for a new wardrobe and taught me how to walk in heels.

Mary was a model. Not the kind that walked around the living room displaying Tupperware in her whore makeup, but the real, professional kind. She worked the trade shows. On any given day she could be found selling cell phones or modeling ball-gags. She was so diverse. She was also beautiful...from afar. What one might refer to as *good from far, but far from good.* She was tall and leggy like Amanda, dense and blonde like Flounder-Tits, and loose in the lips like Jill. So what was wrong with her, you might ask? Well, she looked like Mr. Ed in a wig. She had a big mouth. Not in the 'she gossips too much' kind of way. She just had a gargantuan smile. All teeth and more gum than Bubblicious. It was as if she was actually blessed with two mouths that seamlessly connected in the middle. When she laughed, it

Jen Ashton

echoed before it left her lips. Not to mention, her whole face disappeared.

Despite her major setback, Mary and I hung out all the time. She was entertaining. There was always a story with her. She enjoyed frequenting the local troughs to find men. Currently she was dating three stallions: the magician who wore her bikinis, the celebrity who liked her strap-on and the old man with the big penis. Her sex life was anything but uninteresting. And my lucky ass always got the details first hand.

"So there we were on my couch when my roommate walked in!" she laughed one evening at happy hour. I had to hold on to my seat. She almost inhaled me.

I wasn't sure which beau she was referring to, but any way I imagined it, it was funny. We shared a few laughs, ate a little sushi (their most popular appetizer) and had a few drinks. It was our girl time. No men allowed. Unfortunately, happy hour was usually busy and full men on the prowl. But have no fear, Mary came prepared that day.

"Watch this," she whispered as one unsuspecting douche walked up to our table.

"Hey ladies, mind if I join you?"

"Sure, have a seat," Mary offered politely.

As the meathead—adorned in his size smedium bedazzled shirt—sat down, Mary retrieved a small machine from her purse and pressed a tiny red button on it. A loud, unrelenting fart blasted from its speaker. It sounded wet.

"*Oh my Gawd*!!!" Mary squealed. "Did you just fart???"

There was no denying the sound, only its origin. The poor guy turned red in the face and squeamishly excused himself. Mary giggled under her breath and turned to me. "Works like a charm," she laughed, handing me her device under the table.

"A fart machine?" I asked. "Girl, where'd you get this?"

"The party store. I thought I was pretty funny, too."

That was the beginning of the end. A few margaritas later and Mary and I were in the women's bathroom pushing buttons and laughing our asses off.

Closing the doors to our adjoining stalls, I pushed the *long* version of a double wet fart. It echoed between the tile walls of the restroom where a group of women were standing in line.

"Mary? Was that you?" I called out so everyone could hear me.

"Yah. My stomach hurts. I think I ate something bad."

"Are you okay," I asked, pushing another button. This one blasted short, loud farts.

"No. Don't eat the sushi," she moaned.

We played this game for a good five minutes until I flushed my toilet and walked out. No one would look me in the eye. Apparently, there was something funny they wanted to keep from me. I was washing my hands when Mary finally showed face. The women whispered to one another as she waltzed by, holding her stomach.

"Oh, Jen," she moaned, "I think I might have food poisoning." I pushed the button again. "Oops! Excuse me," she apologized, gazing back at the line of women who looked nothing short of horrified. "I wouldn't eat the sushi, ladies."

And just like that, we left the ladies room with one last fart and headed back to our table.

*****

An hour and three drinks later, Mary was a little tipsy.

"I hope you're not driving," I scorned.

"I'm fine," she assured me, flagging down the waitress. "Um, I'll take one of these mega margaritas."

When her drink arrived, it was so big it came in a mixing bowl. It was the size of a small pond. "Holy shit!" I exclaimed. "I hope you're not planning on drinking *all* of that!"

But she was. And she did. About half way through Lake Margarita, Mary stole my cell phone and starting taking up-skirt pictures of herself. To my surprise—and to the surprise of the patrons at the table next to us that she proudly showed—she wasn't wearing any underwear. And it didn't stop there. By the time the bill came around, she had flashed two bartenders, our waitress, six people at the bar and me. It was time to go.

"One sec," she argued. "I have to finish my drink."

It took me two minutes and all the strength in my body to pry her lips from the straw of that mega margarita. And by the time I did, it was gone. And so was Mary. She took off. Right out the door, into the street, where she continued to run. And run. And run. Who knew that alcohol channeled her inner Forrest Gump.

"Mary!" I shouted at the top of my lungs. "Mary! Come back!"

I chased her down Sunset Boulevard in the middle of Friday night traffic. The cars were bumper to bumper, headlight to tail light, as Mary weaved in between them, seizing every chance she had to moon a driver or buff a hood with her tits. Her halter came down, her dress went up, and the people honked. It was the gig of a lifetime for an amateur model. All eyes were on her.

"Mary!" I called, dodging cars and apologizing to everyone in her wake. "Stop!"

But she just kept running. It seemed nothing could stop her. Except a little thing called a speed limit sign. No, it wasn't the speed limit that stopped her, but the sign. Literally. Mary made a sharp right turn off of Sunset, down the street where we had parked; more than a slight downhill grade. She ran down that road in her five-inch heels with an unstoppable momentum that sent her tumbling head over feet. Rolling like a snowball, she finally came to rest when she slammed into the base of a speed limit sign—where she decided to test out her stripping capabilities.

When I reached the bottom of the hill, Mary had an audience of thrill-seeking tourists, snapping camera phone shots of her dancing on her new pole. "Stop!" I cried out again; this time to the photographers.

Mary heard me and took off again. Right in front of a moving car. The driver slammed on his brakes, coming to a screeching halt an inch from Mary's knees. Like a deer in the headlight, she froze, paused, and—like any frightened mare— pulled down her top and flashed the man's entire family. That was it. We needed to get out of there. Fast. Before we got arrested. I put Mary in my car and we disappeared into the bustling LA night.

*****

As we made our way through the Hollywood hills, Mary said she was feeling sick.

"Can you pull over, Jen? I think I'm gonna puke."

I found a nice neighborhood street and slowed to a stop, parking on an incline.

"You gotta get out," I told her, not realizing her ruse. "I don't want you puking in my car."

Well, she got out. And started running again. *Who the hell was she running from? Me?* I just wanted to make sure she got home safe. I closed the passenger door and followed her with my car. Driving at five miles per hour, I stayed on her heels until she finally gave up. She waved me down and walked up to my driver's side.

"Had enough?" I asked, rolling down my window.

"Yah," she said. "I'm tired. All that running made me have to pee though. Can you wait here? I'm gonna go piss behind that bush."

"Hurry," I replied, looking around to make sure the owners of the house weren't aware that their lawn was being used as a urinal.

A few moments later, a very drunk Mary appeared out of the darkness and joined me in my car.

"Not so fast," I told her as she began buckling her seatbelt. "I'm not driving you anywhere until you get some of that alcohol out of your system."

"How do I do that?"

"Throw up," I insisted.

"I can't just throw up," she argued. "I'm not even sick."

"Here," I offered, handing her a Starbucks straw wedged in my center console. "Use this."

"For what?"

"To gag yourself," I told her.

"I've never done that before."

"Sure you have. You're a model." I handed her the straw and nodded toward her open door. "I'm not leaving until you do it."

Mary tried stabbing the inside of her throat for thirty minutes until I finally grew impatient and pushed her head down on the straw. Ah, success! There was my pretty friend in her halter dress, leaning out of my car puking her guts out. Finally.

"You ready?' I asked as she pulled herself together and wiped her mouth with the hem of her dress.

"Um, not yet," she hesitated.

"Why not?" The look on her face had me worried.

"We can't go anywhere just yet."

"*Because?*" I inquired further.

"Because I didn't pee behind that bush."

I was confused. Okay, so she still needed to piss. No biggy. I could wait a few minutes more while she relieved herself. "So go pee now," I suggested.

"It has nothing to do with pissing, Jen."

"What does it have to do with then?"

"I knew I was too drunk. But I didn't think about gagging myself. I thought running would make me feel sick so I'd have to puke. But it didn't. So when I went behind that bush, I used the garden hose to wash down some laxatives."

Holy Mother Christ!!! Was she serious?!! This girl never ceased to amaze me. Here we were, parked alongside some of California's most pristine homes, in a beautifully landscaped neighborhood, on a Friday night, not a public toilet in sight, and my best friend was about to get a case of the runs. Pre-calculated runs, might I add.

I threw my hands up in defeat and leaned my head down on the steering wheel. It was over. The fun was over. I waved my white flag and let out a deep sigh. "You've gotta be fucking kidding me," I mumbled.

"I'm not," Mary whispered. "Sorry." And five second later, "Oh God, here it comes!"

Mary squatted down behind the passenger door, hiked up her dress and looked me right in the face like a toddler would. The noises coming from between her legs were reminiscent of our old friend, the fart machine. Her cheeks flushed and her brow perspired. She looked scared. I would be too if I was about to unload my ass on someone's front curb. (Wait. Oh, never mind. That was his front *windshield*.) Luckily, we were parked on an incline. I couldn't have planned it better; except maybe I would've called Mary a taxi.

Three, two, one…blast off!

*****

I'd like to say that Mary had her moment and we went wee wee wee all the way home. But that wasn't the case. I sat there in my car, parked in that upscale Hollywood Hills neighborhood, watching my girlfriend shit the street for an hour. One whole hour of horrible, terrible, no good, very bad runs. While she stared at me, and I stared at her, I knew in that moment—definitively—for the first time in my life—that my childhood friend, Jessica The Cowboy (the one who first told me that girls don't poop) was, in fact, full of shit. And so was my friend Mary.

THE END

Girls Don't Poop

Jen Ashton

Also available now:

Turds in the Punch Bowl

by

Jen Ashton

Available through Amazon in paperback and
Kindle
(read on for an excerpt)

I woke up to the unfamiliar sound of thumping against my bedroom wall. Wiping the sleep from my eyes, I rolled over to check the time on the digital alarm clock glowing from my nightstand.

"5:03? Are you kidding me?" I thought to myself as I refocused my attention to the sounds coming from Joe's bedroom. *What the heck is he building now?*

My best friend Joe was notorious for building things. Things and stuff, as I always referred to them. They were never necessarily useful things; however it was typically clever and innovative stuff. He would often get a wild hair up his ass to construct some off-the-wall idea that he dreamt of or saw on TV. Just never at this hour.

Thump. Thump. Thump.

I laid there in the waning darkness of the in between. Moments ago it had been pitch black in my room, a symbol of the night. And now as I lay there tossing and turning under my cool sheets, the sun was peeking its head over the mountains of the east, slowly brightening my room like someone in the sky was turning on the dimmer switch. *Ugh.* I rolled over and covered my ears with the pillow.

Bump. Bump. Bump.

It was then that I heard something peculiar between the thuds echoing through my drywall. *Did my ears deceive me?* I lifted the pillow off my head for a better listen. *No, it couldn't be.* But it was. True enough, the thumping from the other room was in fact Joe's headboard banging against the wall, followed by tantric moans escaping the lips of a woman.

A woman? Joe brought home a woman?

This was a rare feat for the rather tactless and desperate Joe. We had spent the greater part of the last year trying to get him laid, and to no avail.

Jen Ashton

After his divorce, Joe had been enduring a rather painfully long dry spell. We tried countless tactics and rehearsed hundreds of opening lines, night after night, with little to no success. It seemed the scars of his marriage had left a lasting impression on his confidence, rendering him completely useless in the dating pool. No matter how well I prepped him before I sent him out there into the endless abyss of blonde, Vegas bimbos, somehow Joe had a talent for effortlessly torpedoing into an embarrassing nosedive. Crash and burn every time.

Most of his conversations would start out strong. "Hi, my name is Joe." But that's about as far as he ever got on his good foot. From there he would segway into comments such as, "I'm divorced. My wife was a stripper and she left me. I had a kid once, but she wasn't mine. I have three piercings in my penis. Do you want to see?" Almost always in that order, and yes, almost always in one breath.

You get the point. It was no secret that Joe was about as smooth as a serrated knife. Although I was always hiding in a corner watching from afar and laughing my ass off, neither Joe, nor the object of his abrasive introductions were ever smiling when all was said and done. He needed practice and a stern talking to about the stench of desperation.

I explained to Joe on several occasions that desperation was like dog shit; it stinks. Sometimes you don't even know you've stepped in it, but when you do, it lingers. Everyone can smell it. We could wash his old shoes a thousand times, but chances were that a few sneaky remnants of poo would encrust themselves deep into the ridges of his *soul* and remain forever. On this morning, he must've finally decided to change his shoes.

I fumbled in the faint light for my cell phone and dialed our friend Michele.

"Hello?" she answered in a scratchy voice reminiscent of a forty year old smoker.

"Michele!" I shouted in my best whisper-voice. "Wake up!"

"What? What time is it?" she asked, although it was more of a rhetorical question brought on by her grogginess. "Oh my God, Jen, it's 5 o'clock in the morning. What?"

She was half asleep, and although she was on the other end of my phone, I still prompted her to quiet down.

Jen Ashton

"Shhh..." I hushed her. "You need to wake up." I waited a few beats for her to gather her wits and listen carefully. "Right now, right at this very moment, Joey is getting laid!"

There was a long pause as she tried to process the impossible.

"Shut up! Are you serious?" She raised her voice again briefly, but then quieted herself on her own accord as she remembered we were being secretive for reasons still unknown to her.

"I can hear them in the other room as we speak. He's got her moaning like a cat in heat. Get up, I have an idea!"

"Oh lord," she moped. I could hear her rolling over in her bed.

"Michele, get up. Meet me in the party section of Walmart in twenty minutes."

Girls Don't Poop

Jen Ashton

About the Author

Jen Ashton is a successful published artist, #1 Bestselling Kindle Author and entrepreneur with a background in creative marketing and business consulting. Internationally known as "The Artist to the Poker Stars," she paints portraits and collections for athletes, celebrated personalities, and fine art collectors worldwide. Her popular blogs and erotic short stories have generated national attention from a strong web following since 2004. Ashton currently lives in Las Vegas, Nevada with her son and consistently strives to be a positive role model for her family and friends.

To read more books by Jen Ashton, visit her complete library on her Amazon Author page.

To learn more about Jen, visit her online at www.jenashton.com.

For up-to-date news, like Jen Ashton's Facebook fan page:
http://www.facebook.com/jenashtonauthor

or follow Jen Ashton on Twitter:
http://www.twitter.com/jenashtonart

Girls Don't Poop

Jen Ashton

Made in the USA
Lexington, KY
09 August 2012